the
upside

the upside

A Memoir

Abdel Sellou

Preface by PHILIPPE POZZO DI BORGO

In collaboration with Caroline Andrieu

Translated by Lauren Sentuc

Originally published as *You Changed My Life*
(*Tu as changé ma vie*)

SEVEN DIALS

Originally published in English in the US under the title *You Changed My Life*
The second US paperback edition published in 2019 by Hachette Books
Hachette Book Group, 1290 Avenue of the Americas, New York, NY 10104

This edition published in Great Britain in 2019 by Seven Dials
an imprint of The Orion Publishing Group Ltd
Carmelite House, 50 Victoria Embankment
London EC4Y 0DZ

An Hachette UK Company

1 3 5 7 9 10 8 6 4 2

Copyright © Michel Lafon 2012, 2018
Translation © Weinstein Books by Lauren Sentuc 2012

A CIP catalogue record for this book is
available from the British Library.
ISBN (Mass market paperback) 978 1 8418 8354 0
ISBN (eBook) 978 1 8418 8355 7
Printed in Great Britain by CPI Group (UK) Ltd,
Croydon, CR0 4YY

MIX
Paper from
responsible sources
FSC® C104740

www.orionbooks.co.uk

For Philippe Pozzo di Borgo,
For Amal,
For my children, who will find their own way

A Note from the Publisher

This memoir is the unforgettable personal story of Abdel Sellou,
the man who inspired the "Dell" character in the movie *The
Upside*. His story has been retold several times, in various for-
mats and under different titles. The original French version of
this memoir was known as *Tu as changé ma vie* ("You Changed
My Life"), and the original French film based on his friendship
with Philippe Pozzo di Borgo was the international phenome-
non *Intouchables* ("The Untouchables").

Preface

When Eric Toledano and Olivier Nakache were writing the script for the hit French film *Intouchables,* they wanted to interview my special friend Abdel Sellou. He answered: "Ask Pozzo, I trust him." When I was writing the new edition of my memoir, *Le Second Souffle, Suivi par Le Diable Gardien* ("Second Wind, followed by Guardian Demon"), I asked Abdel to help me remember a few of our shared adventures, but he also declined. Abdel doesn't talk about himself. He acts.

With incredible energy, generosity and impertinence, he was by my side for ten years. And in that time he supported me through each painful phase of my existence. First, he helped me with my wife, Béatrice, who was dying, then he pulled me out of the depression that followed her death. He basically helped me find the desire to live again . . .

Throughout the course of these years we've had many things in common: never revisiting the past, never projecting ourselves in the future, and most important, living, or surviving, in the moment. The suffering that was consuming me destroys memory; Abdel didn't want to look back on a youth that I could only guess was turbulent. We were both worn clean of any memory. During all of that time, I only got a few snippets of his story that he was willing to reveal to me. I have always respected his reserve. He quickly became a part of the family, but I have never met his parents.

In 2003, Abdel and I and our unusual relationship were featured on an episode of Mireille Dumas's French television program *Vie privée, vie publique* ("Private Life, Public Life"). Later Mireille decided to make a one-hour documentary about our adventure, which was broadcast as *À la vie, à la mort* (meaning, roughly, "Come what may"). Two journalists followed us for several weeks. Abdel let them know, in no uncertain terms, that probing anyone from his entourage about his past was out of the question. However, they didn't respect his wishes, and as a result, were subjected to an impressive fit of rage. Not only did Abdel not want to talk about himself—he didn't want others to talk about him either!

Everything seemed to change last year. What a surprise it was to hear him answering, with genuine sincerity, all the questions asked by Mathieu Vadepied, the artistic director who filmed the bonus feature for the *Intouchables* DVD. I learned more about him during the three days spent together in my home in Essaouira, Morocco, than I had in our fifteen-year friendship. He was ready to tell his story, all of it, from before, during, and after our meeting.

What an accomplishment to come from the silence of his twenties to the pleasure he gets today in recounting his escapades and sharing his thoughts! Abdel, you will never cease to amaze me . . . What a pleasure to read his memoir. In it, I recognize Abdel's humor, his sense of provocation, his thirst for life, his kindness, and now, his wisdom.

According to his book, I have changed his life . . . That may be true, but in any case, what I *am* certain of is that he changed mine. I will say it again: he supported me after Béatrice's death and helped me find the desire to live again with joyful determination and rare emotional intelligence.

And then one day, he took me to Morocco . . . where he met his wife, Amal, and where I met my companion, Khadija. Since then, we see each other with our children regularly. The "Untouchables" have become the "Uncles."

Philippe Pozzo di Borgo

Prelude

I ran as fast as I could. I was in good shape back then. The chase started on the rue de la Grande Truanderie—Big Cheat Street. You can't make that stuff up. With two friends, I had just relieved some rich kid of a slightly outdated Sony Walkman. I was going to explain to him how we'd actually done him a favor, since, as soon as he got home, his daddy would rush right out and buy him the latest model with better sound, easier functions, longer battery life . . . but I didn't have the time.

"Code twenty-two!" yelled a voice.

"Don't move!" shouted another.

We took off.

Flying down rue Pierre-Lescot, I slalomed between passersby with impressive agility. It was easy—classy, really. Like Cary Grant in *North by Northwest*. Or like that ferret in the children's song, only bigger: he went this way, he went that way . . . Turning right onto rue Berger, I was planning to disappear into

Les Halles. Bad idea—too many people blocking the stair entrance, so I cut a hard left onto rue des Bourdonnais. The rain had made the pavement slick and I wasn't sure who had better soles—me or the cops. Luckily, mine didn't let me down. I was like Speedy Gonzales racing at high speed, chased by two mean Sylvesters, ready to gobble me up. I really hoped this would end like in the cartoon. Now on the Quai de la Mégisserie, I caught up with one of my buddies who'd taken off a split second before me and was a much better sprinter. I raced behind him onto the Pont Neuf, closing the distance between us. The shouts from the cops were growing fainter behind us—it seemed like they were already giving up. Of course they were—we were the heroes . . . still, I didn't risk looking back to check.

I ran as fast as I could, until I was almost out of breath. My feet were killing me so badly I didn't think I could keep it up all the way to Denfert-Rochereau station. To cut it short, I hopped over the short wall meant to keep pedestrians from falling into the river. I knew there was about a twenty-inch ledge on the other side that I'd be able to walk along. Twenty inches was enough for me. I was slim back then. I crouched, looking at the muddy waters of the Seine rushing powerfully toward the Pont des Arts—the pounding of the cops' cheap shoes on the pavement getting louder—and held my breath, hoping the noise would reach its climax, continue on and fade away. Completely oblivious to the danger, I wasn't afraid of falling. I had no idea where my two friends had gone, but I trusted them to find a good hiding place. As the cops ran past, I snorted *oink oink,* snickering into the collar of my sweatshirt. A barge shot out from under me and I almost jumped from the shock. I stayed there a minute to catch my breath. I was thirsty. I would have loved a Coke about then.

I wasn't a hero. I knew that already, but I was fifteen and had always lived like a wild animal. If I'd had to talk about myself, define myself in complete sentences with adjectives, names, and all the grammar they'd tried to hammer into me at school, I would have had a hard time. Not because I didn't know how to express myself—I was always good at talking—but because I'd have had to stop and think. Look in a mirror and shut up for a minute—something that's tough for me even now at forty—and wait for something to come to me. An idea, my own self-appraisal, which, if it were an honest one, would have been uncomfortable. Why would I put myself through that? No one was asking me to, not at home or at school. Incidentally, I was great at handling interrogation. If someone even thought of asking me a question, I took off without blinking. As a teen, I ran fast; I had good legs and the best reasons for running.

Every day, I was on the street. Every day, I gave the cops a new reason to come after me. Every day, I sped from one neighborhood of the city to the next, like in some fantastic theme park where anything goes. The object of the game: take as much as possible without getting caught. I needed nothing. I wanted everything. I was growing up in a giant department store where everything was free. If there were any rules, I wasn't aware of them. No one told me about them when they could have, and after that, I didn't give them the chance. That suited me just fine.

One October day in 1997, I was run over by an eighteen-wheeler. The result: a fractured hip, smashed left leg, intensive surgery, and weeks of rehabilitation in the suburb of Garches. I stopped running and started gaining a little weight. Three years before that, I'd met a man stuck in a wheelchair after a paragliding accident—Philippe Pozzo di Borgo. For a short time, we were equals. *Invalides*—invalids. As a kid, that word only meant a metro station to me, an esplanade wide enough to steal stuff while keeping an eye on the guys in uniform—an ideal playground. I had been benched temporarily, but Pozzo was permanently out of the game. Last year we both became the heroes of a hit film, *Intouchables*. Now suddenly everyone wants to touch us! The thing is, even I'm a good guy in the story. I have perfectly straight teeth, I smile all of the time, have a spontaneous laugh, and I bravely care for the guy in the wheelchair. And I dance like a god. Everything the two characters do in the film—the high-speed freeway chase in a luxury sports car, the paragliding, the nighttime walks through Paris— Pozzo and I really lived it. I didn't do that much for him— at least not as much as he did for me. I pushed him around, acted as his companion, eased his pain as much as possible, and I was present.

I'd never known a man that rich. He came from a long line of aristocrats and had done well on top of that: multiple college degrees and the presidency of Pommery champagnes. I used him. He changed my life but I didn't change his, not very much, anyway. The film made the truth prettier to make you believe in a better world.

—

I might as well say it straight off—I'm not really like the character from the movie. I'm short, an Arab, and not particularly endearing. I've done a lot of bad things in my life and I'm not looking for any excuses to justify them. I can talk about them today thanks to the statute of limitations. I have nothing in common with the real untouchables, those Indians condemned to a life of misery . . . If I belong to any caste, it's the Uncontrollables, and I am their uncontested leader. It's my true nature, independent, rebellious to any discipline, established order or morals. I'm not looking for excuses, and I'm not bragging, either. A person can change. I'm living proof . . .

The other day, I was walking on the Pont Neuf—it was just about the same kind of day as it had been back when I had that chase with the cops. An annoying, icy drizzle trickled down my balding scalp and a cold wind blew into my jacket. I thought it was magnificent—this bridge in two sections linking the Ile de la Cité to the Right and Left Banks of Paris. I was impressed by its dimensions, its width—almost one hundred feet—and its luxurious sidewalks with circular overhangs on the Seine to let pedestrians stop and admire the panorama . . . at no risk. What an idea! I leaned over the edge. The river ran through Paris like a galloping horse, its color like a stormy sky, and looked like it would swallow everything up. As a kid, I didn't realize that even an expert swimmer would have trouble making it out. I also didn't realize that exactly ten years before I was born, the French had tossed dozens of Algerians into these waters. And they did it knowing full well how dangerous the river was.

I looked at the stone ledge where I had hidden from the cops and shuddered at my former audacity. I thought that, now, I'd never dare climb over the edge. I thought above all that now, I had no reason to hide or to run.

I

Unsupervised Freedom

1

I don't remember the town in Algeria where I was born. I have forgotten everything about its odors, colors, and sounds. I only know that when I got to Paris in 1975, at the age of four, I didn't feel homesick.

My parents told me, "This is your uncle Belkacem. This is your aunt Amina. You are their son now. You stay here."

The kitchen of their tiny two-bedroom smelled like couscous and spices, like it did at home. We were just a little more crowded, especially since my brother—one year older than me—also came with the package. The oldest of the children, a girl, had stayed back home. A girl is too useful to give up. She would help our mother take care of the two other children born after me. That way, there'd be three Sellou kids in Algeria, and that was enough.

A new life and the first news flash: Maman is no longer Maman. You can't call her that. Don't even think about it anymore. Now Amina is Maman. She's so happy to suddenly have two sons because she had long worried that their marriage produced no children. She caresses our hair, pulls us onto her lap, kisses our fingertips, and promises us we'll never want for love. Except that we don't even know what love is. We'd always been sheltered, fed, cared for, and held on nights when we were sick, sure, but no big deal—it was just natural. I decide that it'll be the same way here.

Second news flash: Algeria no longer exists. We live in Paris now, on boulevard Saint-Michel, in the heart of the French capital and, yes, just like back home, we can go and play. Apparently it's a little chillier downstairs. What's that smell? Does the sun beat down on the paving stones like it does on the asphalt in my hometown? Do the cars honk with as much enthusiasm? I go to find out, with my brother tagging along. I only notice one thing in the pitifully small park at the Abbaye de Cluny: the other children don't talk like we do. My brother, the oaf, stays glued to me like he's afraid of them. My uncle, the new father, reassures us in our native language. We'll learn French soon enough at school. Our school bags are ready.

"You're getting up early tomorrow, kids. But that doesn't mean you have to go to bed when the hens do. At home, the hens never go to bed!"

"At home, Uncle? But where is home? In Algeria? In Algeria the hens don't go to bed, right, Uncle?"

"Well, they don't go to bed as early as they do in France."

"What are we now, Uncle? Where is our home?"

"You're chicks from Algeria on a French farm!"

Third news flash: from now on, we'll grow up in a country and learn the local language, but we're still, and will continue to be, what we have been since our first breath. All of this is a little complicated for kids, and I've already closed myself off to any intellectual effort. My brother puts his head in his hands and huddles more closely behind me. Man he's annoying . . . as for me, I don't know what French school is like, but I quickly adopt the motto that I'll use for years to come: we'll cross that bridge when we come to it.

I was far from imagining, then, what kind of ruckus I was going to cause in the barnyard. I didn't have bad intentions. There was no kid more innocent than me. Put simply, if I hadn't been Muslim, I would've had a halo.

It was 1975. The cars driving up and down the boulevard Saint-Michel were called Renault Alpine, Peugeot 304, Citroën 2CV "Deux Cheveaux," Peugeot Talbot. The R12s were already old-fashioned and, if I'd had to choose, I would have preferred the 4L, which at least wasn't pretentious. A kid could cross the street unaccompanied without a cop automatically taking him into custody. The city, the outdoors, freedom weren't considered dangerous. Of course we'd run into a drunk from time to time, but we assumed he'd chosen to live that way and so we left him alone. Nobody felt the slightest bit guilty. Even the less fortunate didn't hesitate to toss him a few coins.

In the living room of our apartment, which doubled as my parents' bedroom since we arrived, my brother and I took up all the space, two princes in bell-bottoms and high-collared shirts. On the black-and-white TV screen, a little puny bald guy shook with anger because he couldn't catch Fantômas. In another show, he danced on the rue des Rosiers dressed up as a rabbi. I had absolutely no idea what a rabbi was or what the irony of his situation was, but I still loved the show. The two adults watched their new children laughing in loud spurts. That made them much happier than Louis de Funès's gags and funny faces did. Back in that same time, Jean-Paul Belmondo was running across rooftops in a white suit. He thought he was "*Le magnifique*"—I thought he was nuts. I much preferred Sean Connery in his gray turtleneck. At least his hair never got messed up—he'd pull amazing gadgets from his pockets that got him out of every sticky situation and with exemplary discretion. James Bond was true class. Spread out on the Oriental couch, I savored each and every moment without worrying about the next one and never thinking about the past. Life was as easy as 1-2-3.

In Paris, as in Algiers, my name has stayed the same: Abdel Yamine. In Arabic, the root *abd* means "to revere" and *el* means "the." Revere the Yamine. I nibbled on dates, and Amina picked up the pits.

2

Giving children to a brother or sister who doesn't have any was—and still is—common practice in African cultures, whether they're black or North African. In those families, you're born to a father and mother, of course, but you easily become the child of the entire family, and the family is big. When you decide to give away a son or daughter, you don't really ask yourself whether or not they'll suffer. For the child and adult alike, changing parents is supposed to be something that is simple, natural. There's nothing to discuss, no reason to whine. African people cut the umbilical cord earlier than Europeans do. As soon as we learn to walk, we dive into the unknown and go see what's happening elsewhere. We don't waste time hiding in our mothers' skirts. And if she says so, we adopt another kid.

There must have been two or three undershirts included in the package, but the instructions on how to educate us weren't included. How do you raise kids, talk to them? What do you let them do and what do you forbid them to do? Belkacem and Amina had no idea. So they tried to imitate other Parisian families. What did those people do on a Sunday afternoon back in the seventies, just like they do today? They go walking in the Tuileries gardens. So at the age of five, I walked across the Pont des Arts to hang on to the sides of a murky fountain. A few carp struggled miserably in that two-foot deep swamp—I'd see them come to the surface, open their mouths to suck in some air, and then go right back in for another trip around their bathtub. We rented a little wooden sailboat that I pushed toward the center with a pole. Carried by the current, and provided the wind was blowing in the right direction, the boat could reach the other side of the fountain in just ten seconds. I took off in the direction of the estimated destination, maneuvered the ship's bow, and launched the sailboat again with gusto. From time to time, I looked up and marveled. A gigantic stone arch towered over the garden entrance.

"What is that thing, papa?"

"Uh . . . a very old door."

A door that served no purpose since there was no wall or anything on either side of it. Beyond the garden, I could see enormous buildings.

"Papa, what is that?"

"The Louvre, son."

The Louvre . . . that's as much information as I got. I figured you obviously had to be very rich to live in a house so vast and beautiful with such large windows and statues hanging from its façade. The garden was as big as all the stadiums in Africa put together. Scattered throughout the alleys and on the lawns were tens of petrified men staring at us from on top of their pedestals. They all wore coats and had long, curly hair. I wondered how long they'd been there. Then I went back to my business. With no wind, my boat might get stuck in the middle of the fountain. So I had to convince the other sailors to assemble and launch a fleet so as to create a current and free my vessel. Sometimes Belkacem ended up rolling up his pant legs.

When the weather was really nice, Amina made a picnic and we went to eat on the lawn of the Champs-de-Mars. In the afternoon, the parents laid on blankets. The kids quickly formed groups and started a game of ball. I didn't have enough vocabulary at first and so went unnoticed. I was very nice and well behaved. No different, in appearances, from the little French kids in velvet shorts and suspenders. In the evening, just like them, we went home completely worn out. But no one refused to let my brother and me watch the celebrated Sunday night movie. Westerns kept us awake more easily than the others, but we didn't make it to the end very often. Belkacem carried us to our bed one after the other. For love and devotion, you don't need instructions.

In Algiers, my father went to work wearing cotton slacks and a suit jacket. He wore a short-sleeved button-down shirt and tie and polished his leather shoes every night. I guessed that he must have had an intellectual job that didn't get him dirty, but I didn't know which one and I didn't ask: I truly didn't care what he did. In Paris, my father put on a blue jumpsuit, and a heavy cap on his bald head, every morning. As an electrician, he never experienced unemployment. There was always work, he was often tired, he didn't complain—he joined the daily grind. In both Algiers and Paris, my mother stayed at home to take care of the cooking, the cleaning and, theoretically, the children. But having never set foot in a typical French household, Amina was at a loss to imitate anyone at all. So she opted for doing what they do in her native country: she made us delicious meals and left the door wide open. I didn't ask for permission to go outside, and she wouldn't have thought of demanding any explanations. With Arabs, unsupervised freedom is granted without restrictions.

3

There's a statue in my new neighborhood. The same exact one as in New York—I saw it on television. Okay, so maybe it's a little smaller, but anyway I'm six, I'm tiny, so to me it's enormous. It's a woman, standing, wearing only a sheet, she's lifting a flame to the sky and she's got a strange crown of thorns on her head. I now live in project housing in the XVth district. No more cramped apartment in old, boring central Paris—we're now citizens of Beaugrenelle, a brand-new district bristling with high-rises just like in America! The Sellou family has acquired a first-floor apartment in a seven-story building with no elevator, made of that red brick they call *pierre de Paris*. Life here is like in any other project in Saint-Denis, Montfermeil, or Créteil. Except we have a view of the Eiffel Tower. And by the way, I consider myself to be from the suburbs.

At the base of the tower, they built us an enormous shopping center with everything you need inside—you just have to go down and serve yourself. I don't think I can say it enough: everyone bends over backward to make my life easier.

＝

At the checkout in Prisunic, just within the reach of my little hand, are little plastic bags. And just next to that are shelves stuffed with all kinds of things and candies. I love the Pez candy dispensers, a kind of lighter topped with a plastic head: you push on the lever, the square piece of sugar comes up, and all you have to do is slide it onto your tongue. I quickly get myself an impressive collection. In the evening, I line up my favorite cartoon heroes in order of preference. My brother, that big buzzkill, interrogates me.

"Where'd you get the Beagle Boy Pez, Abdel Yamine?"

"It was a present."

"I don't believe you."

"Shut your trap or I'll punch you."

He does what I say.

I also like boats, submarines, and tiny cars for the bath: you crank a lever on the side that lifts a mechanism and the machine starts going. On many occasions at the store, I fill entire bags with them. First, I go into the store, like all the other people who go to do their shopping, then I unfold a bag, make my selection, serve myself, and leave. One day, it occurs to me that I skipped a step. I should have gone through the checkout, according to the store manager.

"Do you have money?"

"Money for what?"

"To pay for what you just took!"

"What did I take? This? This costs money? What do I

know? And let go of me, first of all—you're hurting my arm!"

"Where is your mother?"

"I dunno, probably at home."

"And where is that?"

"I dunno, somewhere."

"Okay. Since you're playing tough guy, I'm taking you to the *poste*"—the police station.

Now I'm really confused. I know what the *poste* is—I've been there many times with Amina. We buy stamps or rent a phone booth so she can call her cousins in Algeria. What's that got to do with the Pez? Oh yeah, now I get it! At the *poste,* you can also get money. You give a piece of paper, signed with numbers on it, to the lady at the desk, and in exchange, she takes hundred-franc bills out of a little box. I look up at the store manager, who is holding me firmly by the hand—I hate that.

"Mister, there's no point in going to the *poste*. I won't be able to pay you because I don't have the little piece of paper!"

He looks at me stupidly, like he doesn't get it.

"What are you talking about? The police will take care of this, don't you worry!"

So this guy is obviously a complete idiot. There are no policemen at the post office, and even if we found one I doubt he'd pay for my candy . . .

We enter a gray hallway. This isn't the *poste* I know. The people are sitting in chairs against a wall. A man in a dark blue uniform checks us out from his desk. The store manager doesn't even say hello. He goes straight to the point.

"Officer, I've brought you this young thief I caught stealing red-handed in my store!"

Red-handed . . . this guy's watched *Colombo* too many times . . . I pout and tilt my head to the side: I try to look like Calimero, the cartoon chicken, when he gets ready to lisp his famous line: "Ittho unfair. Ith really tho unfair!" The manager makes it worse by presenting my loot to the on-duty officer.

"Look! A whole bag! And I bet it isn't the first time, either!"

The cop sends him on his way.

"Okay, okay, leave him with us. We'll take care of this."

"Well, you make sure he's punished to the maximum! That'll teach him! I don't want to see him hanging around the store again!"

"Sir, I just said we'll take care of it."

Finally, he goes. I stay there, standing, I don't move. I've stopped doing my impression of the poor little victim of an outrageous injustice. In fact, I've just realized I really don't care what happens now. It's not even that I'm not afraid: I don't know what I could be afraid of! There were bags there, just at my height, and candies, too, just within reach, so they should have known I was going to help myself, right? I'm being honest, I thought that's what they were there for—the Carambars, the strawberry Tagadas, the Mickey Mouse Pez, Goldorak, Albator . . .

The cop barely looks at me, takes me into an office where he presents me to his two colleagues.

"The manager of Prisunic caught him swiping from the shelves."

I react immediately.

"Not from the shelves! Just next to the checkout, in the candy!"

The two others smile kindly. I don't know it then, but I'll never again meet such gentle faces in this place again.

"You like candy?"

"Well, yeah, of course."

"Of course . . . so you'll tell your parents to buy it for you from now on, okay?"

"Yes . . . okay."

"You know how to get back home by yourself?"

I nod.

"Well, that's good. Now go."

I'm already halfway out the door. I hear them making fun of the store manager behind me.

"What did the guy think? That we were gonna throw the kid in the slammer?"

꙲

I'm the best. I managed to slip three chocolate-covered marshmallows into my pockets. I wait until I get past the street corner to taste the first one. I still have my mouth full when I get to the door of my building. I run into my brother, who's coming back from grocery shopping with Mother. He immediately suspects something.

"What are you eating?"

"A chocolate-covered marshmallow."

"How'd you get it?"

"Someone gave it to me."

"I don't believe you."

I give him a big smile. All black with chocolate, no doubt.

4

*The French grow up with a leash around their neck. That reas-*sures their parents. They're controlling the situation. At least . . . that's what they think. I watched them coming to school in the morning. The parents would hold their offspring by the hand, they would walk them to the gate, they would encourage them for the day with all of their silly pep talk.

"Work hard, honey, be good!"

They thought they were giving their kids the strength they'd need to survive that pitiless jungle—the playground—where the parents themselves had been hazed thirty years before. But they were only making the children weaker.

To know how to fight, you have to have chosen your weapons. You can never start too early.

I was the smallest, not the toughest, but I always attacked first. I won every time.

"Give me your marbles."

"No, they're mine."

"Give 'em to me I said."

"No, I don't want to!"

"Are you sure?"

"Okay! Okay! I'll give them to you . . ."

The lessons in the classrooms didn't interest me, and the worst thing was, they really took us for clowns. Revere the Yamine, they said. So, what, I was going to be ridiculed, standing in front of the class reciting a story about cows and frogs? That was for the white kids.

"Abdel Yamine, didn't you learn your poem?"

"What poem?"

"The fable from Jean de la Fontaine that you were supposed to learn for today."

"Jean de la Fontaine? Why not *Manon des Sources*?"

"Well, the young man knows Pagnol!"

"I prefer Tylenol."

"Out, Sellou!"

I loved getting kicked out of class. This punishment, the most humiliating of all, according to the teacher, gave me, more than anything else, excellent opportunities to do what I did best. Either the architect of Parisian schools never planned on naughty little Abdel coming along or he decided to make my job a whole lot easier: the coatracks are hung just outside the classrooms in the hallways! And what do you find in coat pockets? A franc or two, sometimes five on a good day, cookies and candy! So getting kicked out of class, well, it was paydirt.

I imagined the kids going home in tears that afternoon.

"Mommy, I don't understand what happened, my coins disappeared . . ."

"Well, once again, you didn't take care of your things. That's the last time I give you any money!"

Yeah right, until next time, and little Abdel's next harvest will be just as good . . .

On my tenth birthday, when the teacher gave me a trip to the hallway disguised as a present, I came across a piece of paper worth a fortune. It had been well hidden under a pink and white handkerchief inside a girl's duffle coat. When I touched it, it was thicker than a bill and bigger than a movie ticket, but I couldn't figure out what I'd found. I pulled my hand out of the pocket. A photograph. It was a photo of the coat's owner, but not just a simple portrait. We call it an American shot: from the waist up. And the girl was naked.

I admit it: if I was ahead of my age for stealing, I wasn't when it came to girls. But still, I immediately saw the advantage to what I'd found.

"Vanessa, dear Vanessa, I think I've got something that belongs to you . . ."

While pretending to pinch my nipples:

"Looks like something's growing, huh?"

"Abdel, give me back the photo right now."

"Oh no, it's much too pretty. I'm keeping it."

"Give it back, or . . ."

"Or what? You'll tell the principal? I'm sure he'd love to see it, too."

"What do you want?"

"Five francs."

"Okay. I'll bring them for you tomorrow."

Our transaction continued for a few more days. Five francs wasn't enough: I asked for more and more. It was a game, I was having a blast, but Vanessa—a bad loser—figured out how to bring it to an end. One evening, on my way back home, my parents grabbed my hand.

"Abdel, we're going to the *poste*."

"To the post office, you mean?"

"No, not the post office. We've been called down to the police station. What have you done?"

"Uh, honestly . . . I don't know . . ."

I knew exactly, but I was thinking of something much more embarrassing than my small-time racket. When the policeman explained the reason for the invitation, I practically sighed with relief.

"Mr. Sellou, your son Abdel Yamine has been accused of extortion of funds."

Those words were too complicated for Belkacem. By the way, they were for me, too, until he pronounced the name Vanessa. I left with the promise of returning the snapshot to its owner the next day. My parents never understood what had happened. They followed me home without a word and never asked any questions. I never got punished, not at home or at school.

Years later, I found out that the school principal had gone to jail. Among other crimes, he'd dipped into the school coffers. Stealing from children—really, you just don't do that.

5

Every morning, I ate breakfast on the way to school. The deliv- erymen set down their crates in front of the still-closed stores and went happily on their way. A plastic sheet was tightly wrapped around each crate. It only took a simple swipe of a fingernail to help oneself. A box of Saint-Michel cookies here, a can of OJ there. I didn't see the harm: everything was there on the same sidewalk, and at my fingertips once again. And honestly, what's one less box of cookies . . . I shared with Mahmoud, Nassim, Ayoub, Macodou, Bokary. I was friends with all the kids from the Beaugrenelle projects and that didn't include any Edward, or John, or Louis. Not because we didn't want anything to do with them, but because they preferred to leave us alone. Anyway, I was more of a solitary leader. It was *whoever likes me can follow*, and when I looked back, I saw that there weren't too many who did.

We hung out on the slab, that concrete space between the towers, just above the shopping center—our playground. We were good-looking, dressed in the latest trends with the right brand names. The Chevignon jacket, the Levi's jeans cut out on the side with the Burberry scarf showing through the slit. The three-stripe Adidas windbreaker (back in style these days, by the way). The Lacoste polo shirt that I was always attached to. Even today, I love the little crocodile on the shirt pocket.

The first time I got caught in a Go Sport store, I had already cleaned it out many times before. There's nothing simpler: I'd go in, I'd choose the clothes I liked; in the dressing room, I'd put them on one over the other and go back out the same way, incognito. Just a little heavier than when I went in. I'm talking about a time when security guards and surveillance systems didn't exist. The jackets hung on hangers with handwritten price tags attached to the buttons. Then one day, supposedly unbreakable antitheft devices showed up. A simple paper clip was enough to unlock them—you just had to come up with the idea, and I was never at a loss for those, just like I was never at a loss for time.

⌒

Early on, I stopped going with my parents on their Sunday outings to the Tuileries, the Jardin des Plantes, or the Vincennes zoo. On Sunday afternoon, I'd doze in front of *Starsky & Hutch* until Yacine or Nordine or Brahim came by to pick me up. We went down to the slab, sort of looked for something to do—a new idea to put into practice.

The shopping center was closed on the Lord's Day. Not convenient for purchases. Then again . . . what was stopping us from going in? That metal door there, it leads into the store, doesn't it? After all, what do we risk?

Nothing.

I could prove it.

⌐

In the Go Sport store, next to the dressing rooms, there's a door with a little sign over it. It says "Emergency Exit" in white letters on a green background. When a seller has to go and get something that isn't on the shelf, he goes through that door and comes back with the piece of clothing in question. I figured out two things from seeing this: first, that behind that door was all of the stock, and second, that the stockroom offered an exit onto the street. Even that idiot Inspector Gadget could have figured this out by himself.

So the issue here is right in front of us: it's a metal door like the ones I've seen at the movie theater exits. Perfectly smooth on the inside, with no visible handle because it has no lock, it's opened from the inside by pushing down on a large, horizontal metal bar. This way, in case of fire, even if dozens of people rush toward it at the same time, they just need to push for it to give way. Go, go, Gadget, chisel: I unblock the opening and wedge my foot in the crack, Yacine pulls hard on the door, and we slip into Ali Baba's cavern.

But wait a minute, what kind of door did we just come through? I've never seen one like this. Whatever, we're not here to see the sights. I tuck the chisel into my jacket pocket, and we start checking out what's available. Most of it is still folded and wrapped up in plastic, which makes it hard to tell if we like it and if it's the right size. Yacine gets lucky.

"Abdel! Check out these pants! Super cool!"

I raise my eyes toward my friend standing in front of me. The jeans do look cool. The German shepherd baring its teeth right behind him, not so much. My eyes move up the length of its leash, hanging from a wrist almost as hairy as the dog. I keep going and reach a square head topped with a cap. SECURITY. So there's no doubt.

The guard grabs Yacine by the collar.

"This way, both of you."

"But sir, we didn't do anything!"

"Shut up!"

He leads us out of the storeroom by a little door on the shopping center side this time, and locks us in the employee bathroom. Click, clack—it's locked from the outside! I laugh hysterically.

"Yacine, did you see that? They're way smart! They planned to use the toilets as a holding cell for thieves caught in the act. Is that space optimization or what?!"

"Stop laughing, we're really screwed."

"No we aren't, and why? We didn't take anything!"

"Because we didn't have time. And we still broke in."

"Who broke in? You? Did you bust that door, Yacine? Of course not, and neither did I! The door was open, and we just walked in!"

With these words, I lift the toilet lid and drop in the chisel.

A few minutes later, the guard comes back with two cops. We give them our version of the story. Not stupid, but unable to prove anything whatsoever, the guard lets the cops go and takes us back out the way we came in.

"FYI, guys, this door is an alarm. When you walk through it, it triggers a red light in the surveillance room."

I pretend to be awestruck in the presence of this new miracle of technology.

"Wow, that's great. That thing must be very useful."

"Very."

The metal door slams behind us. We go back and find the others on the slab, dying laughing.

～

My biggest job, in terms of volume, was before I was ten. I swiped a go-kart at the Train Bleu toy store in the Beaugrenelle shopping center. A real electric car—you could even sit in it! I can still see myself, balancing that bad boy on my head, racing down the steps with the manager on my heels.

"Stop, thief, stop!"

The thing was worth a fortune.

A lot of us tried it out on the slab afterward. It didn't run very smoothly. Honestly, it wasn't worth the money.

6

The die was cast. I couldn't change now. At twelve, there wasn't the slightest chance of me suddenly becoming the model citizen that society was hoping for. All the other boys from the project, without exception, had taken the same road as me and weren't turning back. You'd have had to take away our freedom, everything we had, take us away from each other, maybe, and still . . . nothing would have worked. You would have had to totally reprogram us, like when you erase the hard drive on a computer and reinstall the operating system. But we aren't machines and nobody would have used the same weapon we used—strength, no laws, no limits.

Early on, we understood how things worked. In Paris, in the Villiers-le-Bel suburb, or in Saint-Troufignon-de-la-Creuse, it was the same combat: wherever we lived, we were the wild animals against the civilized people of France. We didn't even have to fight to keep our privileges because, in the eyes of the law, we were like children, no matter what we did. Here a child is considered irresponsible by definition. We find any and every excuse for him. Overprotected, not protected enough, too spoiled, poor . . . As for me, I claim "trauma by abandonment."

Now in seventh grade at Guillaume Apollinaire junior high in the XVth district, I had my first visit to the psychologist. The school psychologist, obviously. He wanted to meet me in person, having been alerted by a transcript already full of suspension notices and unflattering evaluations from teachers.

"Abdel, you don't live with your real parents, correct?"

"I live with my uncle and aunt. But they're my parents now."

"They've been your parents since your real parents abandoned you, correct?"

"They didn't abandon me."

"Abdel, when parents stop caring for their child, they abandon him, correct?"

He better stop with the "correct" . . .

"I'm telling you they didn't abandon me. They gave me to other parents, that's all."

"That's called abandonment."

"Not where I come from. Where I come from, it's normal."

A sigh from the psychologist in response to my stubbornness. I soften up a bit so he'll let me go.

"Mr. Psychologist, don't worry about me. Everything's fine. I'm not traumatized."

"But yes, Abdel, you are, you obviously are!"

"If you say so . . ."

What's for sure is that we all live recklessly, we kids from the projects. There was never any sign strong enough to let us know we were headed down the wrong path. The parents didn't say anything because they didn't know what to say, because even if they didn't approve of our attitude, they were incapable of straightening us out. Most North African and African children experience things as they come, no matter how dangerous they might be. That's the way it is.

The lessons were only heard, not learned.

"You're heading down a dangerous road, young man!" warned the teacher, the store manager, the police officer who caught us for the third time in two weeks.

What did they all expect? That we'd cry out in fear, *Oh God, I've done a bad thing, what came over me, I'm ruining my future!* The future was a foreign concept, impossible to imagine. We didn't think about time, or plan for the things we'd do and those we'd try to avoid. We were indifferent to everything.

~

"Abdel Yamine, Abdel Ghany, boys, come and see. You've got a letter from Algeria."

We didn't even bother to tell Amina that we didn't care. The letter sat on the radiator in the hallway until Belkacem found it and decided to open it. He gave us a meek summary.

"It's your mother. She asks how you are and if school is going well, if you have friends."

I burst out laughing.

"If I have friends? Papa, what do you think about that?"

~

We were obliged to go to junior high, so we went occasionally. We got there late, talked loudly in class, helped ourselves to jackets, pencil cases, book bags. We did it for fun. Everything was for laughs. The fear we saw in the others' faces excited us just like a gazelle's taking off excites a lion. Chasing an easy target wasn't fun. To see them hesitate, though, to see the signs that they'd realized the danger, to listen to them try to get away, to let them think we meant well before attacking . . . we were merciless.

I got a hamster. A girl at school, where I was now in eighth grade, gave it to me (against her better judgment, but nobody else wanted it). Poor thing, she'd spent all her pocket money to buy herself a friend, and when she started to take it home, she was suddenly afraid of getting in trouble . . .

"I shouldn't have bought it. My dad has always said he doesn't want animals in the apartment . . ."

"Don't worry, I'll find him a new home."

This little rat's funny. It nibbles on its cookie without complaining, it drinks, it sleeps, and it pees. My math notebook is soaked with it. For several days, I carry it around in my backpack. In class, it behaves better than me and when it decides to make noise, my friends cover for it: they squeak really well, too. The teacher is surprised.

"Yacine, did you get your hand stuck in the zipper of your pencil case?"

"Sorry, ma'am, it's not my hand, and it really hurts!"

Explosive laughter in the classroom. Even the little rich kids from the XVth appreciate our stunts. Everybody knows the real source of the strange noises coming from my bag, but nobody tells. Vanessa—that girl again—is a softie and worries about the hamster. She comes to see me at recess.

"Abdel, give it to me. I'll take good care of it."

"Honey, an animal like this costs money."

Extorting funds didn't work out for me the first time, so I'm looking to get my revenge.

"Too bad. Keep your hamster then."

Crap, she didn't bite, that bitch! I come up with a devilish idea: to sell her the animal—in pieces.

"Hey, Vanessa, I'm thinking of cutting off one of its paws tonight at the slab, to see if it can run afterward. Want to come see?"

Her blue eyes roll around in their sockets like my underwear does in the washing machine.

"Are you nuts? You're not really going to do that?"

"It's mine. It's my business."

Okay. I'll buy it for ten francs. I'll bring them tomorrow. Don't hurt it, okay?

"Sounds good."

The next day, Vanessa is holding the little round coin in the palm of her hand.

"Abdel, I'll give it to you but I want to see the hamster first."

I open my backpack, she hands me the money.

"Okay, give it to me."

"Oh no, Vanessa! The ten francs is just for the first paw. If you want another, that'll be ten more!"

She brings the money to my building that evening.

"Give me the hamster now. That's enough!"

"Hey sweets, my hamster has four paws . . . But I'll give you the last two for fifteen, you're getting a deal . . ."

"Abdel, you're a real bastard! Fine, give me the hamster and I'll pay you at school on Thursday."

"Vanessa, I'm not sure I can trust you . . ."

She's crimson with anger. So am I, from laughing. I hand her the stinky little furball and watch her walk away. I never would have harmed a hair on that hamster. It died a few weeks later in its five-star cage at her house. She didn't even know how to take good care of it.

From junior high, I was transferred to a vocational school in the XIIIth district, the general mechanics branch. It's called Lycée Chennevière-Malézieux. On the first day, the associate principal gives us a history lesson, and at the same time, a nice little life lesson.

"André Chennevière and Louis Malézieux were two ardent defenders of France at the time of the German occupation during the Second World War. You are lucky to live in a prosperous and peaceful country. You'll only need to fight to shape your future. I encourage you to use the same courage as Chennevière and Malézieux in learning your trade."

Got it. Like those two dudes, I'm going to join the Resistance. I never had any intention of getting my hands dirty. I'm fourteen, no goals to attain, just my freedom to preserve. Two more years to go and they'll have to let me go. After sixteen, school is no longer mandatory in France. But I know that even before then, they will cut us loose.

I have nothing in common with the herd they want me to

graze with. What was that story already that the French teacher told us last year? The sheep of Panurge—that's it! The guy throws one into the sea, and the rest follow. In this pathetic herd, all the students look like sheep. You have to see it. The empty stare, three vocabulary words at most, one idea per year. They've repeated once, twice, sometimes three times. They convinced someone that they were hanging on, eyeing graduation, university, and all the other bullshit. They have basic instincts: to eat and to fuck—there's no other word for it because it's the one they say to each other all day.

Three pitiful girls have ended up here, in this class of degenerates. At least one of them will find herself in the position, more than once, and under more than just one of them . . . I have my faults, but that kind of violence isn't one of them. Thanks, guys, but no thanks. I play elsewhere, and at other games.

7

*We were restless at Beaugrenelle towers. The stores were start-*ing to get seriously equipped in anticipation of our visits: motion detectors, more sophisticated antitheft devices, security cameras, personnel trained to be on the lookout for certain kinds of customers . . . In less than two years, the security had increased so much in stores that we could no longer steal from the source. We either had to give up on the hooded sweatshirts that suited us so well or else go get them somewhere else . . . directly from the wearers, the kids from the rich neighborhoods. The reasoning doesn't lack logic or cynicism, I can admit it now. At the time, I didn't register anything. Once again, I was absolutely incapable of putting myself in another person's shoes. I didn't try; that didn't even occur to me. If anyone had asked me about the suffering of the adolescent who just got mugged, I would have just laughed. Because nothing was serious to me and nothing was serious to the others, especially not the white kids born with silver spoons in their mouths.

Starting in junior high, parents stopped walking their children to the school entrance. As soon as they left their apartment door, the kids became easy prey. We'd see one, all decked out, and we'd be on him in twos or threes, surrounding him on the sidewalk and walking in the same direction as though we were going to school together, as friends. Other people passed us and didn't notice anything strange. I think they even must have thought they were witness to something remarkable: *So this little communicant is friendly with two Arabs! This boy from a good family has the strength of heart not to reject these boys hardened by a life that's obviously very unstable . . .* They didn't hear the conversation going on between us.

"Your shoes, what number?"

"You mean what size? Why do you want to know?"

"Answer!"

"Size forty."

"Forty, perfect! Exactly what I need. Give them to me."

"Well, no, I'm not going to go to school in socks, for God's sake!"

"I have a cutter in my pocket. You wouldn't want to stain your nice blue sweater with nasty little red drops, would you? Sit down here!"

I'd point to a bench, a step, the entrance to a store not yet open.

"Go on, undo the laces, and make it fast!"

I'd slide the Nikes into my bag and leave with Yacine, who, wearing a size 42, had a harder time dressing himself by way of the little junior high schoolers.

~

Sometimes we did use the cutter. But on the jacket, just on the surface, never on skin. We sometimes had to hit. With our fists and feet. That's when the guy didn't give up easy. We thought that was a really stupid reaction. For a pair of shoes, seriously . . . I got caught a few times. Spent an hour or two down at the station and went home just like nothing had happened. The police in France are far from being as terrible as they are in the movies. I never got the yellow pages thrown in my face, not even a tiny slap. They don't hit kids in France; it just isn't done. There was no hitting at Belkacem and Amina's, either. I remember the screams from certain neighbors: those of the son howling from pain when the father whipped his back, of the mother screaming for her son's torture session to be over. I remember Mouloud, Kofi, Sékou, they got their fair share. You couldn't slap them too hard on the shoulder for days after and you definitely couldn't bring it up, couldn't say that you'd heard and understood what went on. Nothing happened. By the way, nothing ever changed. Life before the whip was just like life after the whip. Mouloud, Kofi, and Sékou still kept their spots down at the entrance or on the slab, and they still ran as fast.

~

I take precautions. I get far away from the XVth. Line 10 to Charles-Michel, change at Odéon, and then get off at Châtelet-Les-Halles. It's a melting pot here. Blacks and Arabs, mostly. Some of them think they're American. They stuff themselves with hamburgers to have the same build as breakdancers. You can hear them coming a mile away, ghetto blasters booming on their shoulders. A baseball cap slapped on their head, but turned backward, and they wear pants as big as they can find. They set down the blaster, turn the volume up, and start to move. They put on their show and the volume covers the sound of negotiations.

Everyone's doing their business without worrying about others; I blend into the crowd. I inhale a sandwich, unload a Lacoste jacket, a pair of Westons, nothing bad: drugs are sold somewhere else, out of my sight. That's not my thing, except when it's to sell to the golden boys from the XVIth district looking to spice up their parties. I sell them dried peppers. It doesn't resemble pot at all, in odor or in color. They don't seem to notice; they fork over the cash. I shape a piece of maple bark and make a perfectly presentable bar of hash. I just have to rub it with the real thing, for color and smell, and roll it all up in some newspaper. At the Fontaine des Innocents, a white kid in a blazer shows up.

"You have any, you have any?"

"And you, you have the cash?"

And the transaction is made just like that; the kid doesn't waste any time. I imagine his expression when he opens the package. He'll take out the rolling papers and the tobacco he's stuffed under his mattress; he'll try to crumble the stuff up to roll a joint, and lose some skin in the process. *It's good shit, right, Bernard? Are you kidding, it's bark!*

Parties, or "zulu parties," as we call them, go on in basements. We're all friends, no matter what our ethnic origins are. And because we're friends, we don't really know each other. I know first names, or nicknames, of every person that passes through, like they know mine: Lil' Abdel. That's as far as it goes. I don't know their last names; they've never heard the name Sellou. They call me little because of my size, not my age, fifteen. There are a lot of younger ones here than me, and some really clueless girls. They get off on the danger they sense; they like getting looks from the boys—already strong like men, but they're going to regret it. I watch this little world from close up, but I'm not really a part of it. One night I'm with some punks, outside; another night, it's raining, I do my business in the shelter of underground passages.

"Hey, Lil' Abdel! Got a lead for you tonight. Some girl from Henri IV is having a party at her house, by Ranelagh. Her parents aren't home, you know what I mean?"

"I'm in!"

At these things, we show up, play nice at the party, until one of us gives the signal that it's time to go. Then we clean the place out. At the very least there's always a brand-new video player to swipe. I disconnect the wires, carefully, and roll them up with skill. The little mistress of the house is horrified. *What are my new friends doing? They were so nice just five minutes ago! How could I have known? Those bad guys!* She locks herself in her room. My friends crack up to see me walking down the street, business as usual, carrying a television that weighs as much as I do.

"Lil' Abdel, you're the best!"

~

You know it . . . tonight we're hanging out at the Place Carré, which isn't very well named since it's kind of round, not *carré,* square. Suddenly things heat up between two guys over on the other side, against the wall. Everybody watches from a distance;

nobody gets close. You don't stick your nose in other people's business. Ever. They start to fight. It's the usual.

What's not so usual is the blood spurting out of one guy's neck. And not so usual, the white rice that's coming out of the throat on the dead guy, black. Dead, for sure.

We clear out in a split second like a flock of pigeons taking off. I didn't see the blade that cut into his flesh; it must have been big and solid, and the hand holding it very strong. And determined. That's the reason I never touch hard drugs, whether to take or to sell. That kind of business can go too far. It's funny: me, who's never doubted myself, me who steals without thinking twice, I know I'd never kill someone over money.

The cops will be here any minute. I run as far as possible. All the witnesses from the scene have scattered around the city and its underground. I saw the dead guy's head hanging heavily to his shoulder, almost cut clean off. But no, I didn't see anything.

8

People died in my neighborhood, too, from loneliness and despair, just like they died in the city. They killed themselves, most of them by jumping out of windows. Every time it was a big event. There were hundreds of us in the little Beaugrenelle project, nearly a thousand, and we all knew each other. There was something sensational about one of us suddenly passing away. The old folks who usually stayed cooped up in their apartments came out onto the landing to talk to the neighbors. But in reality, they didn't really say anything to each other. Some just wanted to be seen, show everybody else that they had compassion for poor Mr. Benboudaoud who finally lost it. Others tried to be clever by explaining the reason for the suicide, which they alone understood, of course.

"He couldn't stand living alone anymore, Youssef, he'd been so depressed ever since his wife's death, when was that already?"

"It's been five years, but you've got it wrong, it's not because of his wife that he killed himself."

Silence, suspense, drum roll, the other waits silently for the big finale.

"He killed himself because of his mail."

"Oh really? So what was in his mail this morning?"

"Didn't you notice he was holding on to a letter when he hit the ground?"

It's true. Old Youssef tumbled out of the seventh floor with a notice from the tax service in his hands. Hats off for not letting go of the letter on the way down.

I can still see this other guy, a French guy totally consumed with booze, crushed under the weight of his failure. He lived in the next stairwell with his wife, who was as habitually inebriated as he was. She left him for someone else, and he jumped out of the window. Except this guy lived on the first floor . . . he broke every bone, stayed there, on his back, with an arm tucked somewhere behind his neck, one leg next to his waist, an elbow stuck in his ribs. When they got to him, the medics looked at the broken puppet and had no idea where to start. They put an emergency blanket over him, in shiny gold paper. He died shining, that sucker.

Another one comes back to me, that made us laugh, my friends and me, as much as it grossed us out: Leila, an obese woman who never left her apartment, jumped from the sixth floor. Her body went *splotch* and exploded on the pavement like an overripe tomato. Another love story gone wrong: her man had started carrying on with another woman, in their apartment. Her man who was found partially decomposed, in his bed, the following summer; he'd had terminal cancer and his new girlfriend was gone on vacation. She had the two-bedroom cleaned and still lives there today.

I had bad luck, really, when I think about it: I, who was always out, I, who barely ever ate at home, I was there every time a neighbor committed suicide. Every time, I cleared out fast. The cops were there just as fast to conduct their investigation. Even when I didn't know if they were looking for me, I knew I was better off avoiding them.

∽

They were looking for me for the murder at Châtelet. There were surveillance cameras on the Place Carré, and so the whole thing had been caught on camera, except the quality wasn't the best and made it impossible to identify the murderer. A big black guy, in a coat and tennis shoes, what could be more generic? They recognized me. They knew me pretty well. Each time they caught me, they kept me as long as legally possible before promising that we'd meet again.

We did meet again during a routine ID check, one morning in a suburban train station where I'd just woken up. I almost never set foot in school anymore, and barely at home: I spent my nights in the RER, the train system, like the other kids from the burbs that I hung out with after dark. We messed around until early morning, when the trains started back up, around five or six o'clock. Then we'd go down to the platforms, settle into a train car, and sleep for a few hours. I'd open an eye from time to time and see a guy in a cheap suit and tie, his little briefcase held safely on his lap like he should have it attached to his wrist with handcuffs. Our eyes would meet, and I don't know who was more disgusted. I thought to myself, *Go on, go to work, keep getting up at the crack of dawn to go earn your pathetic salary. I haven't even gone to bed yet.*

I'd go back to sleep, the imprint of the seat fabric on my cheek. I must have stunk, but everything stinks in Paris. A voice over the intercom:

"Last stop, Saint-Rémy-lès-Chevreuse. All passengers are kindly asked to disembark."

A voice in my ear.

"Abdel, Abdel, shit, Abdel, wake up! We gotta get off the train. It's gonna leave for the depot!"

"Let me sleep . . ."

Another voice, harsher, its owner shaking me by the arm.

"ID check. Let me see your papers!"

I finally sat up, and yawned as widely as possible. I thought of checking the time on my watch, but changed my mind just in time. The civil slave in uniform knew I wasn't there for my First Communion.

"I'll have a croissant with my coffee . . ."

"You've got a sense of humor this early, how nice!"

Blasé, I hand over my papers, all in order, of course. Born in Algiers, I had a resident permit that had just been renewed. I'd even started the naturalization process: in the eighties, anyone residing in France for at least ten years could get a red, white, and blue passport. I didn't hesitate. My brother, the idiot, wasn't as proactive with the paperwork: he was sent back to Algeria in 1986. Belkacem and Amina lost a son, probably the one they would have preferred to keep, if they'd had to choose. The other one, they'd have to go pick up at the police station.

"Sellou, CSI wants to talk to you, we're taking you in."

"CSI? What's CSI?"

"Don't play dumb. Crime Scene Investigation, you know exactly what it is."

I knew right away that it was about the murder at Châtelet. The only thing serious enough to require a trip to Ile de la Cité. I knew I wasn't in trouble: I was a witness, that was it, and I didn't know the killer. For once I didn't have to lie. No need to be clever: no one was accusing me of anything. I could tell the exact truth. There was a fight, a stabbing, the guy dropped dead on the ground, the end.

But the beginning of my judicial career.

9

*I've just turned sixteen. A few days ago, I went before a disci-*plinary council at high school to end my career as a mechanic. I'm accused of skipping class and, incidentally, of delivering a right hook to the management professor.

"Abdel Yamine Sellou, you attacked Mr. Péruchon last April 23. Do you admit to it?"

Wow, it's a real hearing . . .

"I admit it, I admit it . . ."

"Well, that's a good start! Can you assure us that you won't do it again?"

"Well that depends on him!"

"No, it depends on you. Can you promise that that was the last time?"

"No, I can't."

A general sigh of resignation from the headmaster. The other jurors don't even raise their eyes from their crosswords. My insolence is just another part of their boring routine.

They've already seen just about everything. I wonder what it'd take to surprise them. I try humor.

"Mr. Director, you're not going to kick me out, are you?"

"Is your professional future suddenly so important to you, Abdel Yamine?"

"Well I mean . . . I'm asking because of the cafeteria. Thursday's when they usually serve fries. I like to come for lunch on Thursdays."

Nobody reacts. Not even the fattest one, the head educational counselor who never gave me the slightest bit of counsel. *Hello! I'm talking about French fries here!* I imagine he's a cartoon character, transformed into an obese wolf, his tongue drooping to the floor, drool running down onto his fat hairy belly, he can't even get himself over to the plate of crispy fries that Little Red Abdel is holding in his hands.

The director cuts off my daydreaming.

"I'm sorry, I'm afraid your culinary argument won't suffice . . . We're going to confer about it, but I believe the issue is fairly cut and dry. You'll be receiving a letter at home in a few days. You may go now."

"Okay, well, see you later!"

"No, I don't think so . . . good luck, Abdel Yamine."

The letter hasn't come to my parents yet, and I didn't warn them. I avoid them completely. I've been free from the school system and my family for a while now. But in the eyes of the law, I can't be questioned without the presence of a legal guardian. A squad car goes to pick up Belkacem and Amina and brings them to 36 Quai des Orfèvres, to the criminal investigation headquarters. They come into the hallway where I'm dozing, spread out over a chair. They look impressed and defeated at the same time. My mother throws herself on me.

"Abdel, what did you do?"

"Don't worry. Everything'll be fine."

My getting kicked out of school won't matter to them. Anyway, they know I barely ever go anymore (except for the cafeteria, of course) and they haven't had any kind of control over me for a long time. But they're afraid of the hearing they've been called to attend. The first time they came to pick me up at the local precinct, it was already too late to change me. This was proof, us here in front of the cops who handle criminals. What they had feared for me for so long, in silence, with the reserve of those who are helpless, might actually be happening.

"Abdel Yamine Sellou, you were identified by surveillance cameras on the Place Carré, in the fourth basement level of the Forum des Halles. A murder was committed on the night of blahblahblah . . ."

I'm already asleep. My parents are staring at the inspector's lips to understand what he's saying better. The word *murder* has an explosive effect on my mother.

"Don't worry, Mom, it isn't me, I didn't do anything! I was just there at the wrong time!"

The officer confirms it.

"Mrs. Sellou, I'm questioning your son as a witness. He isn't accused of murder, do you understand?"

She nods and scoots back in her chair, reassured. I have and will never have any idea what's going through her head, hers or my father's. They don't talk. They won't talk much when we leave the infamous 36 Quai des Orfèvres together. My father will have barely launched into a sermon when we get to Beaugrenelle. My mother will tell him to be quiet out of fear that I'll take off as soon as he does.

For now, I give my version of the story to the inspector: the guys from Les Halles, I'd never seen them before, I don't know their names, I wouldn't be able to identify them. They still don't end the interrogation. They ask me questions about myself, my life, my routine, my friends from Châtelet who aren't really my friends. He gives me his lecture, for the sake of formality. Either he's paid for that, or it eases his conscience. I guess it must make you crazy to be that bad at what you do . . .

"Abdel Yamine, your parents have small incomes and you get a government subsidy to go to school but you never go to class. Do you think that's normal?"

"Uhhhhh . . ."

"On top of that, the money goes directly into an account in your name. It could at least help your parents dress you and keep you fed."

"Uhhhhh . . ."

"Oh sure, you do just fine on your own, right? You act like the little cock of the walk . . . Listen, I'm going to introduce you to a woman, a judge for minors, she's going to handle you until you're legal."

My parents don't react. They have no idea what's going on, but they already understand that nobody's taking their son away. They know I'm not going to get put in a juvenile detention center. They know that I'll get called in to the Palais de Justice every three weeks and that it'll change nothing, absolutely nothing, for me or for them. Youssef, Mohamed, Yacine, Ryan,

Nassim, Mouloud, like practically all of the kids from Beaugrenelle, are monitored by a juvenile judge. Everybody from the
project knows how it goes. My parents must think it's just
what happens to all of us, whether we are the kids of immi-
grants or the French.

The judge comes to see us. She's a short, round woman with a
soft voice, very motherly. She sort of talks to me like I'm ten
years old, but without treating me like a retard. She seems to
want to help me. She sums up the situation without laying on
the drama. That's a first . . .

"You don't seem to like school too much, Abdel Yamine,
right?"

"Not too much, nope."

"I understand that, you're not the only one, you know . . .
But you like to be out at night? They told me you saw something pretty bad at Les Halles, someone got killed right in front
of you."

"Uh-huh."

"So, do you think it's good for a young man of sixteen to
find himself in that kind of situation?"

I shrug my shoulders.

"Abdel Yamine, we're going to see each other again in
three weeks. Between now and then, I'd like you to think about
what you'd like to do. Maybe where you'd like to live. That
way, we can talk about it and see what we can do. OK?"

"OK."

To my parents:

"Mrs. Sellou, Mr. Sellou, let me remind you that this boy

is your responsibility until he's legally adult, which is eighteen in France. Until then, you must guarantee his safety, from himself included. A child isn't a burden, he's a dependent, and when you become parents you have to accept that. Do you understand what I'm explaining to you?"

"Yes, ma'am."

Yes, this time they get it. Not all of it, but they get it. In the street, after spending three hours in the criminal investigation unit with shoulders slumped and eyes misted over, my father gets up the courage to speak.

"Did you hear that, Abdel? The lady said we're responsible for you, so you're going to behave yourself now!"

I also heard the word "burden." I look at this poor man who's hooked up to wires for thirty years. As we cross over the Seine by way of the Pont Neuf—where I have some memories— I think my life's a whole lot more interesting than his. Suddenly my mother raises her eyes to look at me; they're all wet with tears.

"Abdel, they killed someone in front of you!"

"It was nothing, Maman. It was like an accident or like a movie that I could have seen on TV. I was there, but I wasn't part of it, it wasn't me. It didn't do anything to me."

Neither did their sermons.

II

The End of Innocence

10

*I took advantage of my parents' weakness and didn't see any-*thing wrong with it. At six, seven years max, I had said good-bye to childhood and the sailboats in the Tuileries to take a one-way trip to the state of wild independence. I watched, took stock of humanity. I saw that it was just like it is with animals: there's one dominator for many dominated. I figured that with a little bit of the survival instinct and intelligence, you could make a place for yourself.

I didn't realize that Belkacem and Amina were watching over me, in their own way. Whatever you might say about it, they accepted their role with what little they had, and I accepted them. And I called them Papa, Maman.

"Papa, buy me a new comic book."

"Maman, pass me the salt."

I asked them for what I wanted by giving them orders. I didn't know it was supposed to happen any differently. They obviously didn't know it either, since they didn't correct me.

Again, they didn't have the instructions. They thought that loving parents let their kids do anything. They didn't know that you sometimes had to forbid them things and that it was for their own good. They didn't have a good handle on the rules of proper society, the kind that require politeness all the time and emphasize the importance of behaving at the dinner table. They weren't going to teach me these rules, or ask me to respect them.

I came home many an evening with punishment homework. My mother watched me copying tens, hundreds of lines: *I must be quiet and stay seated during class. I must not hit my classmates during recess. I must not throw my metal ruler at the teacher*. I'd clear off a corner of the kitchen table, spread out my papers, and start my writing marathon. Maman, who was making dinner next to me, might dry her hands on her apron, come up behind me, put her hand on my shoulder, and look at my chicken scrawl piling up on the paper.

"That's a lot of homework, huh, Abdel? That's good!"

She could barely read French.

So she didn't read the comments at the bottom of my report card. "Difficult child who only thinks about fighting," "Attends class as though he's a visitor . . . when he attends," "Child in total rejection of the educational system."

She also didn't read the summons from the teachers, the school director, later the junior high principal, the vocational school director. To all of them, I said:

"My parents work. They don't have time."

I forged my father's signature.

Even now, I'm sure that only parents who know the

French school system and have actually gone through it attend the meetings and appointments for their kids. You have to know how school works and accept the way it works to be a part of it. And most of all, you have to want it. Why would Amina want something she didn't even know existed? For her, the roles were clear: Her husband worked and brought home the money. She did the cleaning, cooking, and laundry. School took care of our education. She didn't consider her son's character, which couldn't tolerate any kind of rule. She didn't know me.

Nobody really knew me, except maybe my brother, who was afraid of everything. I used him sometimes, for little jobs that didn't require any courage. Other than that, we barely talked to each other. When he was deported, in 1986, it made no difference to me. I looked down on him a little: he got himself kicked out of the only country he'd ever known over administrative paperwork. You had to be pretty dumb . . . I hung out with pals from the projects. I say pals because we weren't friends. What's a friend good for? Talking to? I didn't have anything to say because nothing got to me. I didn't need anybody.

━━

At home, I didn't open the letters from Algeria. The people who wrote them didn't interest me. They weren't part of my world anymore, and couldn't even remember their faces: they never came to France and we never went there. My parents—Belkacem and Amina—were simple people, but not stupid. They knew we lived better in Paris than in Algiers; they weren't nostalgic about their hometown. They never piled the mattresses on top of the station wagon for the big summer migration. I had three sisters and a brother on the other side of the Mediterranean. They didn't exist for me any more than I did for them. We were strangers to each other. In fact, I was a stranger to the entire world, free as the wind, uncontrollable and uncontrolled.

11

Actually, this judge-for-kids thing isn't bad. Since I don't get my money from the government anymore, she gives me a little allowance. Enough to buy me a kebab and fries and pay for my transportation. Every three weeks, I go to her office and she hands me my envelope. If I show up with shoes that are borderline too small for my growing feet, she adds a few bills. She hasn't figured out that the nicer she is, the more I ask for. And it works! At the worst, she gives me a speech.

"Abdel Yamine, you're not stealing anything, right?"

"Oh no, ma'am!"

"That sweatshirt looks brand-new. It's nice, by the way!"

"My father bought it for me. He works, he can afford it!"

"I know your father is a hardworking man, Abdel Yamine . . . but you, have you found any training?"

"Not yet."

"Well what do you do with your days then? I see that

you're wearing a track jacket and you like athletic shoes. Do you play any sports?"

"Yeah. Kind of."

I'm running. I'm always running. I run as fast as I can to get away from the cops who're chasing me from Trocadéro all the way to the Bois de Boulogne. I sleep in trains in the suburbs, but I don't sleep much. Once or twice a week, I get a room at a Formule 1 hotel so I can take a shower. I only wear new clothes. I leave them behind when I want to change.

Tourists rush to the foot of the Eiffel Tower to take photos of themselves. They stand right on the axis with Trocadéro, click-clack-Kodak, the memory's made and the camera almost put away in the bag: these Americans don't really take care of their toys. They hold their cameras negligently, dangling from their hands, they're loaded down with raincoats, water bottles, bags they wear on shoulder straps that get in the way of their walking. I give a demonstration to the younger kids looking to get into this line of work. I provide their training. I get closer, hands in my pockets, with the innocent, blissful look of a guy taking in the view and, suddenly, as quick as a cobra, I snatch the camera and take off toward the east. I cross the Trocadéro gardens, head down the boulevard Delessert, then the rue de Passy, and disappear into La Muette metro station. By the time the American realizes what's happened and tells the police, I'm back in the neighborhood and the merchandise has already been offloaded. The field is well organized and its headquarters is the Étienne Marcel metro station. There you can always find a taker for a video recorder, a Walkman, a watch, a pair of Ray-Ban sunglasses. I don't bother with wallets; they're not effective enough: since credit cards showed up, people almost never keep cash on them, so it's not worth it. With technological devices, I easily guarantee myself a nice return. And what's more, no labor costs.

The guys that hang around Trocadéro have no common sense. Or they haven't picked a side yet: thieves versus honest people. They're the sons of storekeepers, middle managers, teachers, working-class people, these idiots who only skip classes one day out of two, who are looking for a thrill, but not really sure they want to find it. They're willing to take risks for me, small, brown-eyed, nothing special. They think I'm cool, they're lonely, they'd want to slum it a little, but since they weren't lucky enough to grow up in the projects like me, they don't know the ways to work that we all learn at the foot of our buildings. They act like puppies who run back with the stick their masters threw and pant with their tongues hanging out hoping for a piece of sugar. If necessary, they hit for me. They give me the merchandise that they aren't capable of offloading anyway. They barely expect a thank-you and they don't get a cut. I feel bad for them. I think they're really nice.

12

Once, twice, twenty times I get taken in. It's always the same dance. Handcuffs and a more or less lengthy custody. Today I receive the honor for peeing on a statue of some Marshal Foch on his faithful steed, like Lucky Luke on Jolly Jumper.

"Degradation of public property. In the cell! See you tomorrow."

"My parents are going to be worried!"

"On the contrary, we'll let them know. For tonight, at least, they'll know you're safe and sound."

I get my sandwich delivered right to my new place of residence. I give twenty clams to a cop who looks at me sideways—he's afraid of bad guys. He's going to do my shopping at the corner store. When I don't like his face, I rip him a new one.

"Hey, moron, I told you ketchup-mustard, no mayo! You can't even take an order! This department's seriously screwed with people like you!"

A drunk is sleeping off his wine in one corner of the cell, and an old man is whining in the other. A voice comes from one of the neighboring offices.

"Can it, Sellou!"

"Uh, Officer, sir, your white guy didn't give me my change."

So the voice, now bored, says:

"Rookie, give him his money back . . ."

The other mumbles that he wasn't planning to keep it. I enjoy my meal.

I always operate in the same neighborhood, so I always run into the same officers (more like the same officers run into me!). Over time, we get to know each other; we're almost close. Sometimes they warn me.

"Sellou, watch out, the clock's ticking . . . you know after your next birthday, we can put you away for good."

I crack up. Not because I don't believe them: I do believe them, because they said so. But for one thing, I can't be afraid of something I don't know, and for another, I have every reason to think that prison isn't so bad. And you get out fast. I see it with the Mendy, those groups of Senegalese who like to have their fun with girls. They go down regularly for gang rape. They get six months, tops, come out a bit thicker around the waist, a fresh new haircut, then they get straight back to business, treat themselves to new, young meat. Only once, one of them got three years because he put the girl's eye out with a crowbar. What he did was really bad, but regardless, we know we'll see him again soon. So prison really doesn't scare me. If it were all that bad, the ones who'd already been there at least once would do anything not to go back. Frankly, I can enjoy my sandwich in peace; I don't see any reason to shake in my boots.

Tomorrow I get out, warmer weather's on the way, the girls will be wearing summer dresses, I'll be back on the prowl, nights out with the guys, sleepless nights between Orsay and Pontoise, Pontoise and Versailles, Versailles and Dourdan-la-Fôret. I've got a nice little stash in my bank account. Almost twelve thousand francs. I have a place to crash in Marseille, another in Lyon, and another close to La Rochelle. I'm going to have a nice vacation. After that, we'll see. I'm not thinking any further ahead.

13

I didn't do my eighteenth birthday justice. It slipped my mind.
I was busy with other stuff, probably. But you can be sure the
cops had circled the date on their calendar because when it
arrived they didn't waste too much time in getting ahold of me.
They came at me all at once, when I was least expecting it, even
though I had no reason to run that day. I was just about to leave
for vacation at the beach! My turn to look like a happy idiot:
I didn't know that the tourist complaints that had been piling
up for months could put me away for years. I really lived like a
wild animal, without any notion of time passing. As long as I was
a minor, I couldn't be judged for petty crimes, so they couldn't
sentence me. As an adult, everything changed, and the things I
did before turning eighteen, written in red on my file, didn't play
in my favor. If I'd straightened up after April 25, 1989, my eighteenth birthday, they wouldn't have had anything on me. Completely oblivious, careless—a happy idiot—I kept on doing what
I'd always done, bad stuff, that is, and it didn't last long.

I was walking down the hall of the metro at Trocadéro, a wide and long hall where the wind blows in every season, making the caps on old guys' heads and silk scarves around ladies' necks flap around. I saw a couple coming toward me, both in jeans, him with a camera on a strap around his neck, her in a beige raincoat. I hesitated for a second: was that camera worth it? Nah, I'd already done well for the day, I could call it quits. Lucky for me. The couple was actually two undercover cops. When they got to where I was, I felt an arm slide under my elbow and a hand grab my wrist. In a flash, I was immobilized by four people (where did the other three come from?), forced down on my stomach, handcuffed, and lifted up just as fast, in this horizontal position, heading toward the exit. The whole thing only took a few seconds. A real kidnapping.

Gray concrete, smashed chewing gum, thin legs perched on stilettos, cinched pants resting on leather heels, worn-out tennis shoes topped with hairy calves, a used metro ticket, an old paper tissue, a Twix wrapper, cigarette butts by the dozens . . . now I understand why Superman never flies low. They finally stand me back up.

"I don't know you! Are you new? Why are you arresting me?"

I wait to hear the official reason for my presence in this pretty little police car, all nice and clean. I definitely don't offer up a reason to put me inside if they don't already have one.

"Assault and theft. We saw you yesterday; we even got nice pictures of you. And again this morning, by the way!"

"Oh! And where are we going?"

"You'll see when you get there."

In fact, no, I don't see. I don't recognize this place. They must have built a phony precinct, like the phony betting parlor in *The Sting,* with Robert Redford and Paul Newman. The same dirty walls, the same jaded civil servants typing up their reports on noisy typewriters, the same indifference toward the defendant . . . They set me down in a chair. The person who owns this office is out for the moment, but I'm told he'll be right back.

"No problem, I've got plenty of time . . ."

I don't worry any more than all the other times. I'll get out in a day or two at the latest. Whatever happens, I'll have had a new experience.

"I won't explain the process—you know it!" says an inspector sitting down heavily across from me.

"Well, yeah, you always . . ."

"From now on, you're in police custody. I'll question you and take your deposition. Then I'll send it to the prosecutor, who'll decide whether or not you'll face charges. You probably realize it's more than likely."

"Okay."

Attentively, I watch the couple from the metro walking between the desks. He still has his camera around his neck; she's taken off her raincoat. They don't pay any attention to me. They've moved on to something else, another rascal, another miserable case.

French citizens, tourists, brave people, sleep in peace. The police are working to ensure your security.

14

From the police station, I was transferred to the Palais de Justice. The prosecutor was waiting for me. Our meeting went down really fast.

"I see in your file that you were seen on Tuesday and Wednesday on the Trocadéro esplanade committing several misdemeanors with various tourists: you stole a video camera, a camera, two Walkmen, you committed assault and battery on two men trying to resist you . . . Do you admit to these charges?

"Yes."

"Do you agree to go before the court immediately, with the assistance of a court-appointed attorney?"

"Yes."

He says to the two officers waiting by the door: "Thank you, gentlemen, you can take him down to holding."

The holding cell is in the basement of the Palais de Justice. The light stays on around the clock. They took my watch and shoved me into a cell, and from there, I lost all notion of time.

It didn't seem long or short to me; I wasn't impatient or anxious. The French government kindly offered me a piece of bread, a serving of Camembert, an orange, some cookies, and a bottle of water. My stomach could stand a diet like this. I thought, *Whatever happens, I'll always have food and water. Anyway, I'm not controlling things anymore.* I dozed on my bunk, the third one, just under the ceiling. Strangely, I had everything I needed.

The sounds I'm hearing aren't familiar. Some cry, scream, slam their fists on their cell door: addicts going through withdrawal. You'd think we were in an asylum. The show going on here could make you laugh.

There are two Arabs there, one small and wiry, the other big and fat. The first paces back and forth in the tiny cell, talking to the second, sitting patiently on the bottom bed. The Laurel and Hardy of petty crime.

"This is bad! This is bad! My wife, my sons, they never worked. What're they gonna do without me? If I go down for months, in jail, they won't eat!"

The fat one laughs, but he's a nice guy and tries to reassure the other.

"Come on, don't worry . . . if your wife has to work, then she'll do it! Your kids, same thing! And when you get back home, you'll find your bank account fuller than it is today, you know!"

"Oh, I don't know, I don't know!"

"Why are you here anyway?"

"For a wallet . . ."

Now I can't help bursting out in laughter. I'm eighteen and already into big crime compared to this guy who could easily be my father. I don't say anything. I don't want to make enemies, even weak ones, but I think it's pathetic to get thrown inside, at fifty-five plus, for stealing a wallet. And he's freaking out, too! It's already unbelievable that he's here for so little, but it's insane that he's making himself sick over it. And I can't imagine the French justice system would spend one franc of its tiny budget to sentence a loser like him. Clearly, he's not putting the country in danger, and if prison has the power of dissuasion, it'll definitely work on this type of guy.

We'll find out pretty fast: the door opens and they come to get us for an immediate court appearance. All three of us are going before a judge, but so are a dozen other defendants who join us in the hallway. We climb the stairs together to the courtroom.

I've never been to the theater in my entire life, but I saw plays on television when I was little. "Set design by Roger Harth and costumes by Donald Cardwell . . ." Well, here we are, and I'm ready to do some improv. The staging seems pretty well done, the roles given out judiciously. There's the one who's sobbing to soften up the judges. The one trying to look sorry, as you might at confession, or at least that's what I imagine. The one cringing in pain, or pretending anyway, even if nobody's interested. There's the nonchalant guy, lips pursed, whistling softly between his teeth. Then there's the happiest kid in the class, to the point where you wonder if he isn't a complete idiot—he's thrilled to be here! Then finally, there's me, hands in pockets, stretched out on my bench, pretending to be asleep for the first several acts. With my eyes half-closed, I watch, scrutinize, savor.

I'm filling in the blanks for my inventory of humanity, but I still come to the same conclusion: there are a lot of dominated, a few dominants, and the judges obviously belong to the second group. They're sweating in their black robes, they sigh with each new case, they barely look up to see the defendant coming forward, they yawn during the defense attorney's little speech (to call this pleading a case is an insult to the attorneys I sincerely admire and respect). The head of the court declares the sentence and slams his gavel down on the table.

"Next case!"

He must want to wrap things up fast. I look at him and wonder if it was worth it studying all those years just to end up here, in a dusty courtroom, sitting in an uncomfortable chair, teaching lessons to pre-retirement-age Mohammeds who steal wallets. By the way, what kind of studies do you have to do to get here? The young elite from the XVIth are always talking about "doing law at Assas," a public university. But what is law, exactly? The law, my law, is whatever I decide for myself. I'm eighteen years and a few weeks old, I go around wearing a Lacoste jacket, I pick up girls easily at the parties I crash, I steal one of their daddies' Volvos, go eat seafood in Normandy, leave the car on the side of the road when the gas runs out and hitch back to Paris. I haven't learned anything yet.

A man leaves the courtroom between two policemen, crying like a baby. He's almost out the door and still begging.

"Your honor, I swear I'll never do it again!"

The judge isn't listening. He's already moved on to the next case. It's Mr. Happy's turn, accused of destroying the ticket counter of a metro station by throwing a trash can through the plate glass window.

The attorney jumps right in.

"Mr. President, I ask you to take into account the fact that my client committed this unfortunate act at a time when no RATP employee was sitting behind the window. He therefore knew he would not injure anyone."

"Surely, Counselor . . ."

What, already? Obviously, the judge has forgotten the attorney's name. He addresses the defendant.

"Over the last six years, you've spent more than five years in prison, and always for the same kind of vandalism. Can you explain to me why it is you start up again at every opportunity?

"Your honor, I don't have any family. Life's hard on the street . . ."

"So that's it . . . well, I'm sending you back to get pampered in jail . . . six months at the prison farm."

He practically asks the defendant if that'll be enough. The guy's not just happy now, he's ecstatic.

The old guy who stole the wallet is relaxed. For me, it'll be eighteen months inside, with eight months suspension and immediate incarceration following the hearing. The sentencing only takes a few minutes. I had owned up to all the accusations. But the court doesn't try to find out anything else, and actually, there was probably nothing else to know.

Ten months inside, so not even a year. The sentence doesn't scare me. I'm almost relieved, like the homeless guy looking for a place to stay. As far as I'm concerned, I'm just dreaming of a bed. And to disappear a little. To erase myself, at the least. There's always a mattress for me at Beaugrenelle, and clean sheets scented with lavender or rose, but I've barely set foot in my parents' home in months. Even if I don't show them respect, even if my attitude, on the contrary, shows that I don't care what they think, I still don't walk through their door at dawn, face battered, woozy from the blows given or received the night before. The moment when I pass out is the one when my father gets up. He drinks his coffee at the kitchen table and joylessly gets ready for another day at work—he's old, tired. I've understood how indecent it is to dive into the sheets Amina irons for a long time now.

I can't stand it anymore. I've slept in commuter trains too many times. I'm wiped out. I want a blanket, hot meals. I want to watch *Looney Tunes* every Sunday night on TV. So, here it goes. I'm on my way to Fleury.

15

Welcome to the rest home.

The day starts gently with a news flash. At eight o'clock, a reporter rattles off that a train jumped the tracks in the Doubs region, with four minor injuries and passengers suffering from shock evacuated by rescue workers. Cock-a-doodle-doo. Alain Prost won the Grand Prix in Budapest, Hungary. The weekend weather: sunny skies and scattered clouds in the northeast with a chance of rain, seasonal temperatures. I slowly wake up, the news anchor gets replaced by a bad song from Jean-Jacques Goldman, but I'm not worried. During the course of the day, I'll get treated to *La Lambada,* the summer hit, from what I understand, at least three or four times. At least that's what they're trying to make us think, anyway . . .

The locks fly open. I stretch and rub my neck, yawn wide enough to break my jaw. Won't be too long till coffee; I can hear the cart coming down the hallway. I hold out my bowl, grab my tray, head back to my bunk. It's a commercial break on

Cherie FM. A chorus of girls is excited because shoes are at 199 francs. According to them, "you'd have to be crazy to spend more." How 'bout if I told them I have a ton of ways to not spend anything at all? I dunk my toast, the margarine dissolves and forms tiny yellow beads on the surface . . . Breakfast in bed, what more could you want? Some quiet, maybe. I turn the radio volume down as much as possible—it's going to continue its serenade until lights out. It's impossible to shut it up completely. Liane Foly, Rock Voisine, and Johnny Hallyday are the worst kind of torture for the inmates of Fleury-Mérogis. Like Chinese water torture. You could go nuts if it weren't possible to drown out the asthmatic meowing of Mylène Farmer with the reassuring purr of the television. I'm rich, with more than twelve thousand francs when I got here, and you only need sixty per month to rent a AV set. I treat myself. We get all six channels including Canal+. Now it's time for teleshopping.

Pierre Bellemare wants me to call him. He's trying to sell me a waffle iron. I look around my cell, no need to get up. *Sorry, Pete buddy, but there's no more room for powdered sugar in my pantry*. It's full of cigarettes (for newcomers in need, because I don't smoke) and Pepitos (for snack time). When I need to go shopping, I give my prison ID number, which is the same as my account: 186 247 T. I'm debited directly at the source, with no sales tax, and no withholdings. I improve on the ordinary, but I really can't complain anyway: the day I got here, I was welcomed by Ahmed, a buddy from Beaugrenelle. Since he was about to get out, he gave me all the necessities: a sponge and Saint-Marc detergent, a small, rectangular mirror in a pink plastic frame, soap that doesn't dry your skin out, the AV set for listening to CDs, headphones included, of course, and a Thermos for keeping water cold or coffee hot.

⁓

My world has been reduced from limitless to a few square feet. I still breathe fine all the same. Mid-morning, a guard suggests I get some fresh air. It's not mandatory; I could stay and watch out for deals from the old mustachioed guy on the shopping channel. But no, I like to go outside. It's often a chance to do business. Being weaned off Gitanes can be cruel for the newly arrived smokers. With a little bit of luck, and if they happen to get a sympathetic cop monitoring their break, they might get through one or two, but they're still far from their usual daily dose. We spot the new guys easily: they're wearing the uniform that they got when they arrived; they still haven't had the time or the opportunity to send for their personal clothes. They stand in the secondhand-smoke clouds exhaled by older detainees and dive for the butts they toss with disdain. The negotiation can now begin.

"Hey, I'm Abdel. You want some smokes?"

"Ousmane. Yeah, I want some! What do you want in exchange?"

"Your jacket there—that a real Levi's?"

"It won't fit you, it's too big."

"Don't you worry, I know what to do with it . . . four packs for your jacket."

"Four! Abdel, my brother, you must take me for a jerk, man! It's worth at least thirty."

"I can go up to six. Take it or leave it."

"Six . . . I can make it for three days with six packs."

"Take it or leave it."

"OK, I'll take it . . ."

The transaction can't happen during the walk: against the rules. It'll be finalized later in the day by a tried-and-true system we call yoyo that's tolerated by the guards. Even detainees who aren't involved play along: for one thing, because it's a way to pass the time, and also because everyone needs something at some time—I mean that not playing along means being excluded definitively from our little community. I knot a rag around the cigarettes, attach the bundle to a sheet, slip it through the window, and start to swing it from right to left. When it gains enough momentum, my neighbor can snag the bundle. Then he passes it to his cellmate,who does the same thing, and so on and so forth until the package makes it to the buyer. Then he attaches his jean jacket to the sheet and sends it back to me the same way. Sometimes the sheet gets torn or a clumsy prisoner drops it. If it lands in the barbed wire on the ground, it's lost forever and ever . . . To avoid this kind of thing, we always make sure we don't "room" too far away from our business partners.

Now it's lunchtime. Soon it'll be nap time. Tomorrow, visiting hours. My parents come to see me once a month. We don't say anything to each other.

"Are you okay, son? Are you getting by?"

"Great!"

"And the others, in your cell, they leave you alone?"

"I have a single. It's better for everybody . . . everything's fine, I swear, it's all good!"

We don't say anything to each other, but I'm not hiding anything from them: I lead a nice life at Fleury-Mérogis. We're all the same here. We begged, we stole, knocked people around a little, we dealt, we ran, we tripped, we got caught. Nothing big.

Some brag that they're in for holdups. We don't believe them. The real bad guys live at Fresnes. A guy named Barthélémy boasts about stealing diamonds from the Place Vendôme. Everybody laughs: we know he's in the slammer for swiping a sausage-and-fries sandwich out of the hands of some suit at La Défense. He was sentenced for "moral prejudice."

~

In the afternoon, at exactly two o'clock, I turn up the volume on the radio to listen to the news. I hear that police who were on a raid got trapped by a crazed gunman in Ris-Orangis. Thinking their colleagues had managed to blow down the door of the apartment where the guy was holed up, several heavily armed officers went in through the window. The nut was waiting for them. Being a former security agent, he was heavily armed, too. He shot first. That makes two fewer pigs in the pen. I'm not happy about it, but I'm not crying, either. I don't care. This world is messed up, it's full of crazies, and everything leads me to think I'm not the worst, far from it. I turn down the volume and turn on the TV. Charles Ingalls is sawing wood, his kids run across the prairie, Caroline tends the coals in the little house's fireplace. I drift off . . .

I'm living it up. Fleury is summer camp. Like Club Med, just without the sun or the girls. Those nice counselors, the guards, make sure nothing upsets us. Blows from nightstick,

insults, humiliation, I've seen all that in movies, but none of it
since getting here. And as far as "bending over for the soap" in
the showers is concerned, it's pure legend or fantasy, I don't
know which one. I'm just sorry for the guards, because they're
the ones sentenced to life here. They leave these gray buildings
at night only to go to another that's not much better. The only
difference is where the locks are located: theirs shut from the
inside, protect them from bad guys like us they haven't locked
up yet. Whether in here or out there, the guards live locked up.
The inmates count the days until they get out, the guards count
the years until they can retire . . .

<hr />

When I got here, I counted the days, too. One week was enough
to know it was better to stop, let the time pass, live every second without thinking about the next, like always . . . I became
social, I knew how to earn the esteem of my neighbors. Between
two cells, there's always a hole in the wall about three to four
inches wide and waist high. It allows you to talk, pass cigarettes, and also let your neighbor watch TV if he doesn't have
one. All you have to do is set a mirror on a stool so it reflects
the image. The other guy has to watch in an uncomfortable
position, his eye glued to the hole, and he has to lean his ear in
to hear the dialogue, but it's better than nothing. Every first Sat-
urday of the month Canal+ shows a porno. A few minutes
before it starts, all the inmates drum on the doors, on tables,
on the floor. Not to demonstrate some irresistible need to
escape, for sure. So why? I don't know. I join in on the noise
like everybody else. I crack up listening to the others, even if I
wish they'd shut up most of the time. Fleury-Mérogis is never

quiet. Never. Except during the monthly porno. As soon as it starts, nobody makes a peep.

I figured out how to get away from the ambient noise by making my own music. It's inspired by films mostly. *Once Upon a Time in the West* came out two years before the blessed Abdel arrived on this Earth. Luckily, my favorite western comes on TV a lot and I never miss it. I learned the lines by heart: "I asked you to scare them, not kill them!" The cold reply from the other: "You're a lot more scared when you're in pain." Or this one: "I saw three coats like this one at the train station this morning. In each coat was a man. And in those three men, three bullets." The coolest! Sometimes I come across one of the silent films with Charlie Chaplin and laugh so hard that the guards worry about my mental health. I laugh almost as hard when I listen to the news on the radio or the TV. In Creil, three girls showed up at school wearing full veils, and suddenly the French think they're in Iran. They're panicking. The news is so pathetic, you're better off taking it as a joke.

It's already evening. The light and the TV go off by themselves after the second movie. It's already the end of the year, and I've pretty much done my time if you consider the suspension period. I must have gained twenty pounds lying around all year like an old pasha. It doesn't look so good on me, but I'm not worried. I know business is waiting for me on the outside, and I'll have to get back on top of my game, start right away, run fast and far. I'll lose the weight. In June, I confessed to everything I was accused of because I thought I'd see daylight a lot sooner if I went straight for the truth. In reality, I could have just denied it, and they'd have let me out on parole until my court date. Maybe I would've disappeared, hidden out at a friend's or with family in Algeria. But I would've been wrong, because then I would have missed out on an interesting and not at all traumatizing experience.

~

On November 9, while I am lying on my bunk, I hear TV newswoman Christine Ockrent say that the wall that has divided Europe for twenty-eight years is coming down. All the news programs are repeating it over and over: the Iron Curtain is falling. Soon I see footage of people prying away cinder blocks and crawling over ruins. An old man is playing the violin in front of some graffiti. The East and West were totally separate from each other until now. It wasn't a story made up by Hollywood screenwriters, and James Bond, if he existed, would really fight Soviet spies . . .

I wonder what planet I was living on before Fleur-Mérogis. Shut up in my cell for the last six months, I have discovered the world. Ridiculous, I know. Here the guards call me "the tourist" because I take everything so lightly. I have that casual look like the guy who's just passing through.

By the way, I've done my time, I'm out of here. Thanks guys, I had a good rest. Here I am, ready to dive back into the big bath of whatever. In Berlin, at Trocadéro, Châtelet-les-Halles, in the basements of Orsay, it seems like everywhere it's the same dump. And if I have to go back to Fleury, well . . . I'll go back.

16

It only took me a few weeks . . . just a handful of days and nights and I didn't have time to get bored. As soon as I got my shoelaces and watch, I was back in business. There were more and more portable CD players around near the Eiffel Tower, and some truly inspired engineers had worked hard to perfect the quality of video recorders, which were, by the way, lighter and lighter. In Algeria, the Islamic Front was starting to ruin all the fun; my brother, Abdel Ghany—Belkacem and Amina's other "son"—took advantage of it to come back to Beaugrenelle. He hadn't gotten his papers, but he needed to make a living: I took him on at Trocadéro. There I found out some guy named Moktar had helped himself to my turf. I smoked him out with the help of some faithful allies by letting him know he needed to be gone, pronto. Moktar got to my brother and used him to scare me. Always the chicken, Abdel Ghany warned me: either I gave up the turf, or he'd get the brunt, my sweet brother. He hadn't come back to Paris for this . . . I thought about my favorite movie, *Once Upon a Time in the West*: intimidate, don't assassinate . . . I chose from my African network, the tallest, the thickest—the best armed—Jean-Michel. Together we paid a visit to my rival. The latter was surrounded by ten of his goons, some who'd worked for me in the past, and a cute brunette.

"So Abdel, that's how you come to see us, alone? Are you suicidal or just crazy?"

"I'm not alone, see?"

Jean-Michel takes out his BB gun and all of the peons disappear, all except for the girl, who's now curious. We left Moktar in his underwear, shaking with fear and cold in the middle of the Droits de l'Homme esplanade. I've described how people calmly changed platforms when a fight broke out in the metro. There at the Palais de Chaillot, they backed up the same way, barely surprised by the show. The girlfriend followed us. We never saw Moktar again.

I'd just gotten out of prison. I was legal, I was responsible, in the eyes of the law, for everything I did. For the first time in my life, there was no more judge, no counselor, no teacher, no parents. No more adults reaching out their hands to try to guide me and filling my ears with their good advice. If I had wanted to be the new Abdel after my stay at Fleury-Mérogis, I would have had no problem finding someone to help me. I'd just have had to ask. Belkacem and Amina didn't turn their backs on me: when they came to see me in the visitation room, just before I got out, they gave me a hard talking to, just like parents should when their son screws up. I waited for their speech to fizzle out . . . I was still oblivious.

My heroes always came out on top. Terminator got hit, but he kept standing. Nobody could beat Rambo. James Bond dodged bullets. Charles Bronson barely cringed when he was hit. It's not that I identified with them: I just saw life like a cartoon. You fall off a cliff, you're flat as a pancake, you get back up. Death doesn't exist. Worst-case scenario, a bump pops up on your forehead and stars circle your head. You bounce back fast from everything, and then you make the same mistakes all over again.

I didn't do anything differently. I reclaimed my turf at Trocadéro. I didn't notice that the cops were keeping an eye on me, and once again, I never saw them coming. Are we going back? Okay, let's go.

17

France is a marvelous country. It could have given up, consid-
ered me a lost cause to myself and everyone else and let me sink
into delinquency. Instead it decided to give me a second chance
to behave like an honest young man. I took it. In appearances,
at least. France is a hypocritical country. As long as you're dis-
creet, it lets every kind of fraud, rip-off, and traffic slide. France
is accomplice to all of its worst citizens. I took advantage of
that, shamelessly.

A few months before the end of my sentence, an educational counselor got interested in my case. He came to see me,
all friendly, and offer me a way out that didn't include theft and
assault: a profession. Where school failed, Justice and its special emissaries thought they could succeed.

"Mr. Sellou, we're going to find you an internship. Starting next month, you'll leave Fleury-Mérogis and go be transferred to a semi-free center in Corbeil-Essonnes. You'll need to
go to your place of work every day and go back to sleep at the

house every evening, except for weekends, when you can go back home to your family. We will evaluate your situation several times throughout the course of your internship and then decide what happens next."

Amen. What the counselor wanted, I could pretend to want, too. But in reality, I didn't see myself sticking to any protocol for one second. You'd have to be pretty naïve, really, to think that a kid who never obeyed his parents, or his teachers, or the cops could suddenly think that obedience was the key to his salvation! What arguments did anyone provide to make me believe that, anyway? None! That said, this white dude in his suit and tie was right to save his spit . . . I listened closely to his little speech. I heard the word "free." There were four letters before that, S-E-M-I? Those I forgot right away. I also heard that I'd be sleeping where I wanted on the weekend. That meant I'd leave Corbeil-Essonnes Friday morning and not come back until Monday evening. Four days in the wild . . . I signed up right there and then.

~~~

Three weeks after the internship starts—in electrical work, just like Papa!—the counselor calls me in.

"Mr. Sellou, is there a problem with your training?"

"Uh, no . . . I don't know."

"Well, I'm told you haven't been in four days."

I figure it out immediately. I never went to see how to handle cables, switches, and circuit breakers. I sent a friend instead. Same height, same build: he looks like me, and I never look like myself in photos. It works like a charm until the friend skips the training . . . he might have at least told me! I'm gonna have to set him straight. In the meantime, I owe the counselor an explanation. I try to get around the issue.

"Actually, I didn't really like the ambience, you know . . . When you start hearing racist jokes . . ."

"Well then, what do you plan on doing? If you stop attending your internship, I won't be able to keep you in the semi-free program. You'll have to go back to Fleury-Mérogis."

Ooh . . . this whitey thinks he can scare me! He doesn't know that the bedding is softer at Fleury than in Corbeil! I swallow my pride, try to look contrite and beg him.

"Give me one week to find another internship. Please, sir . . ."

"One week, not a day more."

Hey, hey! He thinks he's a tough guy on top of it!

"One week, I promise."

What bothers me about Corbeil is that that there's no TV in the rooms. We get back at nine o'clock at the latest, sign the register in front of the uniformed guard with an expression that's so alert, you'd think we were in Saint-Tropez . . . The next day, the doors open at dawn to let the brave get back to the grind on time. In between, there's nothing to do. Nothing, not a thing.

I scoured the classifieds. A chain of pizza restaurants was looking for delivery boys. I'd already stolen enough motor scooters to master the art of driving and I'd run through the streets of Paris enough to know each neighborhood like the back of my hand. I got the job. For a few days, I loaded the cal-zones on top of the moped, I rang doorbells, furious when nobody would buzz me in, mixed up door codes, rescued my double cheeses from crooks that refused to pay, offered margheritas to the homeless guy on the corner. I managed to get a glowing report that I handed to the education counselor with an angelic smile.

"Bravo, Mr. Sellou. I encourage you to keep trying."

"No problem. I've even decided to move on to more serious things."

He's amazed.

"What do you mean, Mr. Sellou?"

"Well . . . I mean that I have ambition. That I won't keep delivering all my life. I've already started helping out the manager."

"Well, good luck. From the bottom of my heart, good luck."

He doesn't think I'll go very far.

18

I played the model employee to earn confidence from management. They showed me how the chain operated, from the order stage all the way to the client's door and on to calculation of the day's receipts, every night, before closing. I moved up fast in the store that hired me. I watched closely and remembered every weakness in their system: despite appearances and the so-called lesson learned in prison, Lil' Abdel hadn't changed. He was just looking for a new way to do business.

After getting caught again at Trocadéro, I understood that I'd have to move to another business. Paris had changed since the mid-eighties and my beginnings in the watch and camera trade. Security had beefed up so tourists could take better, safer advantage of their visits, and the police, even if it had taken them a while, quickly caught on to crooks like me. And it was getting tense between traffickers, who were always wanting more. Drugs were now the best way to make a lot of money. The network created every kind of greed, and guns started showing up. We weren't yet seeing guys walking around with Kalashnikovs like dogs in the projects—that's the norm these days—but gangs were forming little by little and they were looking for any way possible to make an impression on the others. You had to defend your territory. The North Africans didn't really mix so easily with the blacks anymore. The rise of the INF in Algeria scared the French. Newspapers reported their barbaric acts. People started looking down on us and treating us almost like savages. I really did need to find a new orientation, fast.

At Corbeil-Essonnes, I meet a druggie in the semi-free program, like me. He stole a Citroën AX to go to work. Every morning, for two or three weeks, he drops me off just outside of Paris. Then he disappears with the car. I have to take the RER again. I find myself in the place of the honest, hardworking folks who watched me sleep, spread out on the seat, just two years ago.

In his store in the Latin quarter, Jean-Marc—the manager—doesn't know what to do anymore. His delivery boys come back often on foot with their pockets empty. They swear they were mugged in a building entrance. More like they sold the moped, often in exchange for hash, kept the money, and shared the pizzas with their friends. But how could you prove it? Jean-Marc's no fool, but he has no way to take action. You can't fire a delivery guy because he was mugged. You don't file a complaint against him just because you don't believe him. Jean-Marc sighs deeply and asks headquarters to send him new mopeds ASAP. I don't join in on the pathetic business with the rest of the team, I don't say anything, but it can't keep going on like this. I'm coming up with a new plan and these little small-time thieves are preventing me from putting it into action. I talk to the manager.

"Jean-Marc, your guys there, they're making a fool out of you."

"I know Abdel, but my hands are tied!"

"Listen, it's really very simple. It's ten o'clock. Call them, one by one, and tell them you don't need them today. Same for tomorrow and the next day. And in three days, you send them a pink slip for unjustified absence, or something like that."

"Okay, but who's going to make the deliveries in the meantime?"

"I'll find you some people."

If police are sometimes incapable of stopping crooks, it's because they don't use the same methods. They don't anticipate the crime, they don't see the hit coming, they're not on a level playing field. Personally, I'm equipped to deal with these guys. Obviously: I'm one of them! They grew up in La Chapelle, Saint-Denis, Villiers-le-Bel, Mantes-la-Jolie, wherever. We all went to the same school. It's called life in the projects.

I knew how to clean house. Just like magic, those delivery boys don't claim getting mugged anymore; the receipts come back intact every evening. They're delivered by Yacine, Brahim, and a few other future accomplices. They're already playing along; they behave themselves for a few weeks. They know they can trust me to improve things soon. In the meantime, they stuff themselves with pizzas and they're already happy!

There was a TV series I loved when I was a kid: *The A-Team*. In the pizzeria scam, I'm Face, the good-looking one who does everything right, and Hannibal, the one who ends every episode with the famous phrase: "I love it when a plan comes together." I start replacing Jean-Marc on his days off. And when upper management gives him another store, I take his place, with everyone's congratulations. The coast is clear.

In 1991, all the accounting is still done on paper, by hand. In my little pizzeria, we use what we call masters, which are stubbed books of numbered pages that come in double. You slide in a sheet of carbon paper and that way you get a copy of the order. One copy is a receipt for the client, and the other goes back to the main office, which then knows what's been sold and therefore how much a store is supposed to have made.

My plan is very simple: to sell undeclared pizzas. When a client calls to place an order for two or three pies, you just have to ask if he wants a receipt. When it's a small family or two or three students, we don't even ask. When it's a delivery to a company, we systematically provide a receipt. That night, I slip carbon copies of the receipts and their corresponding invoices into the envelope headed for the main office. The rest is for us.

Of course, I also have to justify the use of supplies. Nothing could be simpler. Every morning, when a supplier delivers the dough, the crates of ham and liters of tomato sauce, I give him free coffee. In the meantime, Yacine and Brahim discreetly take whatever we need for our phantom pizzas from the truck. Another proven method: fake orders, all recorded in the master, of course. I pretend that a little joker named Jean-Marie Dupont from Saint-Martin calls to order himself a dozen extra-large pizzas of every combination. Except at that the address he gives, the delivery boy finds a dentist's office where nobody's ordered anything. Obviously, no one delivered anything and the pizzas were never made. Except upper management, after receiving my report, files it unknowingly in the losses column.

⌇

Two guys come to see me at the store.

"We have a proposition for you: we have an empty store nearby. We buy a pizza oven, a moped, we hire a delivery boy. When you get calls here, you send them to us and we take care of the delivery. We split, fifty-fifty."

We invested a small fortune in equipment, registered the business with the chamber of commerce, I put a girlfriend at reception, and we were off. We made a bundle of cash very quickly and then, suddenly, it slowed down. So the idea came to me to type the company name into the Minitel. I found out they opened a second store without telling me. I had the keys for the first one. I went one night, took out the oven—a Bakers Pride worth thirty thousand francs—took the mopeds, and resold everything in parts. My partners had nothing on me: we never signed any contract, my name wasn't anywhere on the documents. They went out of business just after that.

⌇

My friends and I, we were pretty happy with ourselves. We didn't need much. The category of small-time crooks suited us just fine. We weren't looking to make millions, we didn't really think we were smarter than anybody else, we had fun playing pranks on people where no one really got hurt. In our little group, nobody drank, nobody took drugs. We didn't need any useless baggage. Most of all, we knew none of us would ever kill for money and we didn't want to be in the hardened-criminal category. We were looking for fun in all its forms. We got girlfriends from our clientele. After closing up, we'd head to the college girls' places for part two. Between us, we had a competition going: who could get the prettiest girl. It was hot in those tiny studio apartments under the roofs of Saint-Germain. Brahim had his technique: he pretended to be clairvoyant and predicted the girls would fail their finals. He was hoping to console them. His strategy didn't always work. Messengers of bad omens don't go over well with intellectuals. Personally, I made them laugh. You know what they say about a woman who laughs.

I had a hard time getting up in the morning and thought I must be pretty stupid to keep torturing myself like this. Work is tiring. Whether you do it legally or not, it's tiring. I was starting to get fed up. I was afraid of ending up just like the honest people I considered total morons. And on top of that, the pizzeria chain was starting to equip each store with a computer. That was the end of trafficking orders. I asked to be let go. I left to go to the unemployment office with my work certificate. Without making the slightest effort, I was going to get an amount close to my official salary for two years. I had no problem taking advantage of the system.

At that point in my life, I really was like Driss, my character in the film *Intouchables*. Careless, joyful, lazy, vain, explosive. But not really mean.

III

Philippe and Béatrice Pozzo di Borgo

19

Serving hamburgers. Carrying crates from the truck to the warehouse, from the warehouse to the truck. Starting all over again. Filling a tank, giving change, pocketing your tip. When there is one. Guarding an empty parking lot at night. Trying not to fall asleep, at first. Then, sleeping. Observing that the result is the same. Entering bar codes into a computer. Planting flowers in roundabouts. In spring, replacing the pansies with geraniums. Trimming back the lilacs just after they bloom ... I tried a ton of small jobs for three years. Strangely, I didn't discover my vocation. I went to the unemployment office when they called me in, the same way I went to see the judge when I was sixteen to eighteen. Appearing docile and obedient was the unavoidable condition for getting unemployment checks. From time to time, you had to provide something extra. Proof of your good intentions. Nothing big. So, serving hamburgers ... Place the slice of meat between the two pieces of bread. Press the mayonnaise distributor. Go light on the mustard. I handed in my apron fast. I awarded myself a family-sized helping of fries, covered the potatoes with a blob of ketchup—they stank like stale grease—and left giving a huge smile to the whole team.

～

I was supposed to look for a job. I looked very little and did it badly on purpose—that gave me a lot of free time. Day and night, I kept partying with friends who had the same kind of lifestyle . . . random. They worked for four months, the minimum requirement to qualify for unemployment; then they showed up at the unemployment office and got along nicely for a year or two. None of us did anything bad anymore, at least not much. We did sometimes invite ourselves onto a work site at night to goof around with a backhoe, or organize a scooter rodeo in the Bois de Boulogne, but nothing that would disturb the peace. We went to the movies. We snuck in through the exit and left before the credits. Still, I'd almost become a good guy. To prove it, I gave my seat to a pretty mother who was bringing her son to see *Robocop 3*. The kid was wearing nice leather high-tops, American style, and had big feet for his age. I wanted his shoes. I almost asked him where he got them. It didn't even occur to me to take them. That got me worried: *So, Abdel, you getting old or what?* But then I thought, *I don't really need those shoes . . .*

～

The summons to the employment agency got sent to my parents. I'd find the mail balanced on the radiator in the entry where, a few years back, there were letters from Algeria. Communication between my birth country and me had been cut off for a while. It had gotten tense with Balkacem because of the political climate in Algiers. When he watched the news, my father shrugged his shoulders, sure that the journalists were piling drama onto the situation. He didn't believe that the intellectuals were gagged; he didn't believe in the tortures, the disappearances. I didn't even know there were intellectuals there. And by the way, what was an intellectual anyway? Someone who thought well? A professor? A doctor? And why would you kill a doctor? Belkacem and Amina turned off the set.

"Abdel, did you see? You got a letter from the employment agency!"

"I saw, Maman, I saw . . ."

"And? Aren't you going to open it?"

"Tomorrow, Maman, tomorrow . . ."

There was only one envelope on the radiator, but two different summonses. One urged me to go to Garges-lès-Gonesse, where, if I was lucky, I'd become a security guard at a minimart. I don't get it. Garges-lès-Gonesse—is that a new metro station? Did they dig it while I was at Fleury? Ah, no, I see the postal code, in small print between parentheses: Garges-lès-Gonesse (95). There must be some mistake. I specifically told the employment agency that my job search was limited to the beltway around Paris. I crumple the paper into a ball, shove it in my pocket, and check the address on the other paper: avenue Léopold II, Paris XVIth. Well there you go! That's more like it! Old Leo's neighborhood. I knew it like the back of my hand. *Follow the guide. Accessed by two Line 9 metro stations, Jasmin and Ranelagh, the area is home to city mansions and buildings constructed in*

grand style . . . People didn't live in apartments here, they lived in vaults. You can fit twelve people into a toilet; every room has an en suite bathroom; the rugs are as soft as the sofas. In this neighborhood, with no shops, you see little old ladies in fur coats who have their lunch delivered to their doors by the very best caterers. I know that because Yacine and I used to entertain ourselves by cutting off the delivery personnel (who were sometimes little old ladies themselves—we nicely offered to carry their load and then took off with it). We had the commendable intention to create a gourmet food guide, but before doing that we had to taste everything! We tested Fauchon, Hédiard, Lenôtre and even fish eggs from I-can't-remember-where. Don't take us for bumpkins: we knew those little jars were worth gold and contained caviar. "Caviaaaar," as the locals called it. Honestly, it was nasty.

So, here I am on the way to avenue Léopold II . . . I don't even look at the description of the job they're telling me to try for: I already know I won't get it. I just want to get the summons signed so I can prove I really did show up. I'll send it back to the employment agency saying, alas, once again they didn't want me. Life is hard for youth from the projects, you know . . .

~

I'm standing in front of the door. I back up. I step forward again. I put my hand on the wood, carefully, as if it might burn me. Something's weird. It's like the entrance to a castle. Lower the drawbridge! In a minute, I'll hear a voice through the wall. It'll say: "Be on your way, peasant! The lord doesn't give alms. Be gone before I throw you to the crocodiles!"

Is Abdel Yamine Sellou going to make movies? It seems that way, because I feel like I'm taking on the role of Jacquouille la Fripouille in *Les Visiteurs 2*. That's me, the visitor. I look for hidden cameras behind the cars parked along the sidewalk, perched on the shoulders of contracted cameraman. I'm happy in my little daydream. I look like a real whackjob there on the sidewalk . . . *It's okay, Abdel, relax.* Still, I realize I probably shouldn't have thrown the other summons away, the one for Garges-lès-Gonesse. I have to at least send a signature to the employment agency . . . I check the name of the street. It's the right one. Then I check the building number. That's right, too. But still, something's off. Unless . . . wait! Don't tell me they've sent me to the rich people to do housecleaning!

I look at the summons again and read the job title: "Life auxiliary to a tetraplegic person." "Life auxiliary"—what does that mean? I remember them talking about the auxiliary verbs "to be" and "to have" at school. Did "life auxiliary" combine the two? Was this about being and having? It was a strange term. Sounded like I was being recruited by a sect. I could already see myself in the lotus position on a bed of nails, meditating on my path and my salvation . . . and tetraplegic? I'd never seen that word. Made me think of Tetris, or tartare, like the meat, or of magic, or logic. But there wasn't any logic to this.

I touch the wooden door again. I need to feel it to believe it. I'm tiny by comparison. You could stack three of me one on top of the other and still pass through it, and at least twenty-five of me side by side! I look up a little and see a tiny button embedded in the stone and a screen a few square inches in size. An intercom trying to go incognito. I press it, hear a click, and then nothing. I press it again. I talk to the wall.

"The listing for the job, the assistant and everything, is this the place?"

"Come in, sir!"

Another click. But the huge door doesn't move. Am I supposed to pass through it or what? I press again.

"Yesssssss?"

"You know Casper the Friendly Ghost?"

"Um . . ."

"Well, I'm not him! Come on now, open up!"

Click, click, click. Finally, I get it. Like any self-respecting castle, there's a secret passage . . . and I find it! A human-sized door is barely visible inside the giant one. I step forward, grumbling. Here we go, the interview hasn't even happened yet, and I'm already annoyed. This better not take too long. Whoever the dude in here is, he's going to have to sign my paper in double time!

20

Whatever was strange outside was strange inside, too. I walked through the door and into a desert. A hall like this at Beaugrenelle could have been the rec room for the entire project. But here, nothing, nobody. Not one dude to hold up the wall, or roll himself a blunt. The building concierge came out of his office.

"What is this regarding?"

"Uh . . . For the terter . . . the terra . . . For the tartarpegic?"

She gives me a threatening look and, without a word, points her finger at the door at the end of the hall. *Ding dong,* another click, but this time the door opens all by itself. I close it behind me. And the hallucination continues. Someone's playing a joke on me, I'm the victim of a hidden camera sketch. Allen Funt is going to step out and slap me on the shoulder.

It suddenly dawns on me that I'm not at the headquarters of some big company, but in a person's private residence . . . The apartment entrance must be 360 square feet. It opens onto two rooms: on the right, there's a desk where I see a man and a woman, both sitting, probably talking to another candidate, and on the left, a sitting room. Well, I call it a sitting room because there are sofas. There are also tables, dressers, mirrors, paintings, sculptures . . . and even some kids. There are two of them, all nice and clean, the kind I didn't like to share the benches with at school.

A lady passes through with a tray. Some guys are sitting there, uncomfortably, in cheap suits with folders on their laps. As for me, I've got my crinkled envelope in my hands, I'm wearing worn-out jeans and a jacket that's seen better days. I look like a degenerate from the suburbs who just spent a week outdoors. Actually, I hadn't. Yesterday I spent the night at my mother's. I look like I always do, actually. Sloppy, I-don't-care, antisocial.

A blonde comes over to me and invites me to wait with the others. I sit at a huge table. When I put my finger on the wood, a print shows up and then disappears after a few seconds. I look around. As long as I'm here, I might as well do some recon for stuff that could be useful. But I'm quickly let down: no TV, no VHS player, not even a cordless telephone. Maybe over there, in the office? I lean back a little in my chair, wedge my fist under my chin, and start to doze.

Every seven or eight minutes, the blonde reappears and asks the next person to follow her. Each time, the guys look at each other and hesitate, nervous. My stomach is rumbling and I was planning on meeting up with Brahim to eat something, so I interrupt the hello-my-name-is thing and hold my palm up to the indecisive candidates:

"I'll just be a second."

I beeline for the office, the blonde on my heels, unfold the employment agency paper, and put it down on the desk. However, the blond hesitates to sit down.

"Hi," I say. "Can you just sign here, please?"

I've learned to be polite, because it saves time. They look like they're afraid of me. Neither the secretary nor the guy sitting next to her bats an eyelash. He doesn't get up to say hello but I'm not surprised by his rudeness: I've already had interviews with condescending types who treat me like a dog. It's routine.

"Relax, it's not a holdup! I just want a signature, there."

I point to the bottom of the paper. The man smiles, watches me in silence. He's funny with his little silk scarf that matches the pocket on his houndstooth blazer. The girl asks me a question.

"Why do you need a signature?"

"For unemployment."

I'm blunt, on purpose. It's clear that Missy and me are from different worlds. Finally, the other one speaks.

"I need someone to accompany me everywhere I go, including travel . . . are you interested in traveling?"

"What? Are you looking for a driver?"

"A little more than a driver . . ."

"Well, what's a little more than a driver?"

"Someone to accompany me. A life auxiliary. It should be written on your paper, isn't it?"

The weirdness continues. I have no idea what he's talking about. I'm sitting here across from a man in his forties, who is clearly loaded, surrounded by an army of assistants in skirts, I imagine the kids I saw in the sitting room are his and that he has a beautiful little wife, too. Why would he need somebody to hold his hand when he travels? In fact, I still don't see the problem and I don't want to stick around to find out. But I took the trouble to come here, used up all of my brainpower to get into the place, and I'm not leaving without that signature.

"Look, I already accompany my mother to go grocery shopping . . . so come on, sign there, please?"

The secretary sighs, but he doesn't. He looks like he's having more and more fun and takes his time. You'd think this was *The Godfather* when the big boss explains the way things are to the younger bosses wanting to take his place. He speaks calmly, almost fatherly, and with endless patience. "Listen, son . . ." That's it . . . the guy living in this palace is a godfather. Don Vito Corleone is sitting there, across from me, explaining things to me calmly, teaching me a lesson. All that's missing is the plate of noodles and the red-checkered napkin around his neck.

"I have a problem: I can't move by myself outside of this chair. Actually, I can't do anything by myself. But as you can see, I'm surrounded by help. I just need a strong boy like you to take me wherever I want to go. It pays well and offers separate accommodations in the building."

I hesitate . . . but not for long.

"Honestly, I have a driver's license, but I don't know anything about how to . . . The only thing I've driven up until now is a moped with a pizza strapped onto it. So why don't you sign the paper for me and see about all of that with those others waiting in the sitting room. I don't think I'm the right person for you."

"You're not interested in the apartment?"

He touches a soft spot. He sees a vagabond, a little Arab who's never taken out a lease in a neighborhood like this one, a young guy without the slightest ambition, a lost cause. And still, he doesn't know I've done time . . . Don Corleone has a heart. He doesn't have any arms or legs anymore; that doesn't bother me. But heart, I don't have any, not for other people and not for myself. I don't see myself like others see me. I'm perfectly happy with the way things are. I understood I'd never have it all, no matter what I did, so I gave up trying. A bank clerk adores his quartz watch, an American tourist loves his video camera, a teacher cherishes his Renault 5 car, a doctor lives for his suburban home . . . When they get robbed, they're so scared they practically hand you the keys to the safe instead of defending themselves! I don't want to live for any of that. Life's just a giant rip-off. I don't have any possessions, nothing matters to me.

"I'm not going to sign your paper. Let's give it a try. If you like it, you stay."

Only this guy didn't live for anything, either. He'd already lost everything. He could still buy himself everything, obviously, except for the most important thing: freedom. He still smiles. I feel something strange building inside me. Something new. Something that stops me in my tracks. Right there. That shuts me up. I'm astonished, there, that's it. I'm twenty-four years old, I've already seen everything, understood everything, seriously don't care about anything, and for the first time in my life, I'm astonished. Come on, what can I lose by helping him out? One or two days, long enough to understand what I have to do . . .

I stayed for ten years. There were departures, returns, periods of doubt, too, when I was neither here nor there, but in all, I stayed ten years. And there was every reason for it to go wrong between Count Philippe Pozzo di Borgo and me. He came from a long line of aristocrats, and my parents had nothing; he'd gotten the best education available, and me, I quit school in ninth grade; he talked like Victor Hugo, but I got straight to the point. He was trapped inside his own body, whereas I moved mine all over the place without thinking. Doctors, nurses, nurse's assistants, everyone around him looked down on me. For them, who'd made careers out of devoting themselves to others, I was a freeloader, a thief, a troublemaker for sure. I had crept my way into this helpless man's life like a wolf in a sheep's pen. I had the fangs. I couldn't bring good to the table, not a chance. All the warning signs were there. It could only go wrong.

Ten years. Crazy, right?

21

The accommodation suited me fine. You could get to it by one of two ways: either from Pozzo's apartment by passing through the garden or from the building's parking garage. So I was independent. I could come and go—go, mostly—without being seen. Smooth white walls, a small shower, a kitchenette, a window onto the garden, a good mattress and box spring: I wasn't asking for anything more. I wasn't asking for anything more because I wasn't planning to stay.

When handing me the key, the secretary warned me, "Mr. Pozzo di Borgo has also decided to give another candidate a chance. For the moment, you have use of the studio. But if you leave, please be kind enough to leave him the place as you found it."

"Right, I'll be kind enough . . ."

That blonde's gonna have to learn to talk to me with a different tone of voice, or we're not going to get along.

"Rendez-vous tomorrow morning downstairs at eight o'clock for the bath."

She's already gone down two floors when I react. I yell over the bannister.

"Bath? What bath? Hey! I'm no nurse!"

As soon as I'm up, stomach empty, the pattern of the sheet still on my cheek, yesterday's socks on my feet, I find out what a tetraplegic is: a dead guy with a head that works. He asks me questions.

"How are you, Abdel? Did you sleep well?"

A talking puppet. They haven't asked me to help, yet. Babette, a mama from the West Indies at five foot two, all boobs and muscles, takes care of him with precision and energy. She activates what she calls the "transfer machine." It takes forty-five minutes to get the body from the bed to a special shower seat made out of plastic and metal, with holes all over it. Then, after drying and dressing the guy, just as long to get him to his daytime chair. One night at Fleury, I watched a modern ballet. It was just as long and just as boring.

The puppet motivates his troops.

"Okay, Babette, put the Pozzo back!"

The Pozzo. The thing. The animal. The toy. The doll. I watch the whole thing without lifting a finger. Just as frozen as him. I add on to my inventory of humanity. But this guy's in a separate category, with the very special cases. He watches me watching him. He doesn't look away. Sometimes his eyes smile; so does his mouth.

"Abdel, shall we have breakfast at the café afterward?"

"Whenever you're ready."

I catch my reflection in the bathroom mirror. I look pretty rough. And not in the mood to chat. People see me and cross to the other side of the street. The Pozzo finds this hilarious.

━━

We sit on the terrace, under the brazier. I sip my soda quietly, waiting for the next step.

"Abdel, could you help me drink my coffee, please?"

I dream up a cartoon superhero—SuperTetra. He looks at his cup, it floats up to his mouth, he opens his lips, and it tips. He give one quick blow and, abracadabra, the liquid is just the right temperature. Nah, the kids aren't gonna like it. Not enough action. I stow my idea and grab the coffee myself. But I change my mind just as fast.

"Sugar?"

"No thank you. On the other hand, a cigarette would be nice."

"No, I don't smoke."

"Well, I do! And could you please get me one!"

He laughs. I really look like an idiot. Luckily I don't know anyone around here . . . I put the filter between his lips, activate the Zippo.

"What do we do about the ashes?"

"Don't worry about it, Abdel, I'll handle it . . . Pass me the newspaper, please."

Apparently, the *Herald Tribune* is part of the morning ritual because, just before we left, the blonde slipped it into my hands without him asking. I set it on the table. I take a gulp of soda. Tetraman doesn't say anything. He smiles, unblinking, like the day before during my "interview." I finally figure out something's wrong, but I don't know what. He enlightens me.

"You have to open the paper and put it in front of me so that I can read it."

"Oh, right! Of course!"

The number of pages, columns, and the words in each column scare me a little.

"You really going to read all of that? And it's in English, too—that takes a long time!"

"Don't worry, Abdel. If we're late for lunch, we'll run back."

He dives into his reading. From time to time, he asks me to turn the page. He leans his head and the ash from his cigarette falls, just next to his shoulder. He handles it all right . . . I look at him like he's an alien. A dead body disguised as a live rich man from the XVIth. A head that works by magic, and more curious than strange because this head doesn't work like any of the others I've known from this milieu. I like rich people because we rip them off but I hate them because of the world they're a part of. They usually have no sense of humor. Philippe Pozzo di Borgo laughs constantly and at himself more than anything else. I've decided to stay two, three days tops. I'll need some more time to unravel this mystery.

22

I've said that Fleury-Mérogis was like summer camp for me. I'm
stretching it a little. It's true the guards acted like mothers to
the detainees, that sexual violence didn't exist inside those
walls, that exchanges were made fairly and not as a kind of
extortion. But I'm downplaying the negative aspects of prison
a little. During the first days, they stuck me in a cell with two
other guys. Promiscuity was the only thing I couldn't stand. I
could accept having my freedom taken away, eating out of a
metal bowl like a dog, having the toilet in my room and the odors
that go with it. On the condition that the odors were mine.

My roommates decided, *That young one there, we're
gonna get him into line fast* . . . I warned them just as fast. They
had to tear me off them or there would've been broken bones.
They didn't listen to me: one of the guys took a trip to the ER
in Ivry. Considering I'd only defended myself against two pairs
of arms full of bad intentions, management, eager to erase the
incident as fast as possible, gave me a single cell. From that

moment on, the guards acted like mothers to me because I behaved myself like a good boy. In the courtyard, during our walk, I stayed mostly in the middle, at a safe distance from the walls where the druggies in withdrawal and the depressives negotiated their trade. The yoyo system wasn't any good for sheets of pills—too light. So these guys took the risk of doing business in the yard—they didn't really have a choice. A voice boomed out from the speaker:

"You in the yellow and blue jackets, next to the pillar, separate immediately."

In prison, voices boomed out from everywhere, all of the time, though the cells were soundproofed: your neighbor had to turn the TV volume all the way up to bother the others. Strangely, the cries of men traveled through everything. I say that the guards played mother and the guys respected each other because I didn't see anything else. But I heard.

I like the sounds of the Beaugrenelle projects, the kids who hang out on the pavement and the concierge who sweeps the cigarette butts. Frrrrt, frrrt . . . I like the sounds of Paris, the mopeds that sputter, the metro that comes up to street level at Bastille, the whistles from the scalpers and even the screaming sirens from the police cars. At Philippe Pozzo di Borgo's, I like the silence. The apartment looks onto a garden that's invisible from the street. I didn't even know something like that could exist in the middle of Paris. After his coffee, he uses his chin to operate the mechanism on his chair and goes over to the bay window, where he stays for at least an hour. He reads. I discover the indispensable toolkit of the tetraplegic: a portable reading lectern. You stick the book on it—a thousand-page brick with no pictures, printed in small letters, a veritable weapon of self-defense—and a strip of Plexiglas turns the page when Mr. Pozzo tells it to by moving his chin. Staying there is part of my job. There's no sound. I sit down on a couch, I sleep.

"Abdel? Hello, Abdel?"

I open an eye, stretch myself.

"Is the bedding no good up there?"

"Yes it is, but I went to see some buddies last night, so I'm catching up a little . . ."

"Excuse me for disturbing you, but the machine turned two pages at the same time."

"Oh, well that's no big deal. You missing a part of history? You want me to tell you about it? It'll save you some time!"

I'll do just about anything for a laugh. I like to be paid to sleep, but if I have to choose, I'd prefer to be paid to live.

"Why not? Abdel, have you read *The Roads to Freedom* by Jean-Paul Sartre?"

"Of course, it's the story of little Jean-Paul, right, that one? So this little Jean-Paul, he goes for a walk in the forest, you see, he picks some mushrooms, he sings like this, a little like the Smurfs, la-la, lalalala . . . and suddenly, he reaches a bend. So he hesitates a little before going on, of course, because he doesn't know what's after the bend, right? Well, he's wrong, you know, because what's around the bend, Mr. Pozzo?"

"Well, I'm asking you, Abdel!"

"There's freedom. That's it. That's why it's called "The Roads to Freedom." End of chapter, that's it, now we close the book. Come on, Mr. Pozzo, let's go for a walk."

This guy has unbelievably white teeth. I can see them really well when he laughs. They look like the tile in my shower here.

23

I don't remember deciding to stay. Or signing a contract, or of having said *hey, high five!* to the one who became my boss. The day after my arrival, and after that first bizarre bathing session and then the coffee with the *Herald Tribune*, I went back home to change my underwear and get a toothbrush. My mother laughed.

"So, son, are you moving in with your girlfriend? When are you going to introduce us?"

"You're never going to believe it: I found a job. Food and a place to live! With rich people on the other side of the Seine."

"With rich people! Now, you're not doing anything bad, right, Abdel?"

"Well, you're not going to believe that, either . . ."

In fact, I don't think she believed me. I took off to find Brahim, who was now working at the Pied de Chameau restaurant (yes, Brahim also became a good boy). I told him about

Philippe Pozzo di Borgo, his physical state and the place where he lived. I barely exaggerated.

"Brahim, you can't believe it: at this guy's place, you squat down, you pull a string between the slats of parquet, and a banknote comes out. I could see the franc signs appearing in his eyes, like gold bars do in Uncle Scrooge's."

"Come on, Abdel . . . you're kidding! That's not true."

"Of course it's not true. But I'm barely exaggerating, I swear!"

"And the dude, he doesn't move at all?"

"Only his head. The rest is dead. Gone. Kaput."

"But his heart still beats, right?"

"I don't even know. In fact, I don't know how a tetraplegic works . . . I mean, yeah, I do, I know that it doesn't work!"

I can't remember the first days at avenue Léopold II very well, probably because I was there off and on. I wasn't trying to please anyone and definitely not trying to make myself indispensable. I didn't stop for one second to think about the situation, or about what a job in this house with this strange handicapped man could bring me, or what I could bring to this family. Time had maybe done its work on me, like it does on any person, but I wasn't aware of anything. I'd already had pretty varied experiences and had learned some things from them, but I hadn't put all of it together, not out loud and not in my head. Even in prison, where the days are long and, you'd assume, ripe for thinking, I numbed my brain on television and news radio. I didn't have any fear of tomorrow. At Fleury, I knew the near future looked like the present. There was nothing to worry about on the outside, either. No danger on the horizon. I had so much self-confidence that I knew I was invincible. I didn't *think* I was invincible: I *knew* I was!

They put me in a police van to take me from the courthouse on the Ile de la Cité to Fleury-Mérogis. It's a van equipped with two rows of narrow booths in the back. Only one detainee per booth because you can't fit it any more than that. You can stand up or sit down on a board wedged in sideways. The handcuffs stay on. The door is part solid, part wire mesh. You don't look out the window: you've got this web of steel threading in front of you, a narrow passage and then another booth holding another guy headed for the same place. I didn't try to make out his face in the darkness of the van. I wasn't particularly crushed, though I was not very happy either, of course. I was absent from the others and from myself.

The superheroes from the movies don't exist. Clark Kent doesn't become Superman when he puts on his ridiculous costume. Rambo doesn't feel the blows to his body, but his heart is in tatters. The Invisible Man's name is David McCallum; he wears Lycra undershirts and has a really bad bowl cut. But I didn't know my own weakness. My gift? Insensitivity. I wasn't born with it. I was able to spare myself all unpleasant emotions. I was a human fortress inside, impenetrable. Superman and his colleagues were nothing. I was convinced that the world counted on real, and rare, superheroes and that I was one of them.

24

Madame Pozzo di Borgo's first name is Béatrice. I like her from the start—she is open, simple, not prudish. I call her "Madame." It suits her well.

But this morning Pozzo tells me, "Madame is going to die soon."

His wife is sick. Some kind of cancer. When he had the paragliding accident that put him in his present state two years ago, they told him that he could expect to live seven or eight more years. The big bonus: he might be the one to live longer.

In this house, there's no partitioning of family on one side, personnel on the other. Everyone eats together. We eat on pretty normal dishes—I know they don't come from the local supermarket but, still, they go in the dishwasher. Céline, the children's nanny, takes care of the cooking. Very well, by the way. The kids don't ask her for much more. Laetitia, the oldest, is the typical spoiled-rotten adolescent. She blows me off superbly, and I try to do the same to her. Robert-Jean, twelve, is the picture of discretion. I don't know which of the two is suffering more from the situation. To me, rich people's kids have no reason to suffer. I want to shake that bratty girl whenever I see her. Show her what real life is like so she'll stop whining for two seconds because the bag she's been eyeballing for weeks isn't available anymore in caramel brown. I'd like to take her for a tour of Beaugrenelle for starters, then we'd go full on, to the projects in Saint-Denis, to the squats in abandoned warehouses where you find not only druggies in withdrawal but also families, kids, babies. No water, obviously, no heat and no electricity. Filthy mattresses lying directly on the ground. I wipe the sauce with a piece of baguette. Laetitia picks at her food—she's left half of the veal. Béatrice gently scolds her son for picking out the slices of onion. He tries to regroup them, with the tip of his fork, into a corner of his plate. Soon Béatrice won't be strong enough to sit at the table with us. She'll be lying down in her room, here in the apartment or in the hospital.

You've got to admit it . . . these aristocrats are magnets for bad luck. I look around me. The paintings, the marquetry furniture, the Empire dressers with fine gold handles, the half-acre garden in the middle of Paris, the apartment . . . What good is it to have so much if you're not alive anymore? And why is it bothering me?

―

The Pozzo is in pain. The Pozzo takes some painkillers. The Pozzo suffers just a little less. When he's better, I take him to Beaugrenelle. We don't get out of the car. I lower the window, a friend tosses a small package onto my passenger's lap, and we leave.

"What is this, Abdel?"

"Something to make you feel better that actually works. Not sold in pharmacies."

"For goodness sake, Abdel, you're not going to leave it there! Hide it!"

"I'm driving. I can't exactly let go of the steering wheel . . ."

The Pozzo doesn't always sleep at night. He holds his breath because breathing hurts; he inhales air suddenly and it's even worse. There isn't enough oxygen in the room, or the garden, or in the tank. Sometimes they wake me up: you have to take him to the hospital, right away, without delay. Waiting for an ambulance equipped to transport a tetraplegic would take too long. I'm already ready.

⸻

The Pozzo suffers most from seeing his wife in such bad health and from being helpless against her illness, like he is against his own handicap.

I tell jokes, I sing, I brag about made-up things. He wears support hose. I slip one on my head and imitate a holdup.

"Stick 'em up . . . Stick 'em up, I said! You, too!"

"I can't."

"Oh? Are you sure?"

"Sure."

"That's a bummer . . . well, I want the most valuable thing in this stinking house. Not silver, not paintings, no! I want . . . your brain!"

I jump on Pozzo and pretend to cut open his skull. It tickles him. He begs me to stop.

I slip on one of his tuxedo jackets, too big for me, punch

the top of his Stetson to make into a bowler hat, and walk around his bed whistling a ragtime tune, imitating Charlie Chaplin in *Modern Times*.

Why do I bother? I don't care about these people. I don't know them.

But then again, why not? What does it cost me to clown around either here or back in the projects? Most of my friends are starting to get themselves together, like Brahim. I don't have anyone to go hang out with. It's nice and warm here, the decoration is nice—it has potential. Potential for pleasure.

The Pozzo's body is hurting. I have the decency—what is happening to me all of a sudden?—not to ask why. The other trial-basis candidate pacing around the chair is praying furiously. He keeps a Bible in one hand at all times, looks up to the sky, forgetting that the ceiling is in the way, he says words ending in -*us* like in the Astérix comics and even chants for a cup a coffee. I pop up behind him singing Madonna.

Like a virgin, hey! Like a vir-ir-ir-ir-gin . . .

This candidate, Brother Jean-Marie of the Assumption of the Holy Trinity of the Cross of Notre Dame of the Blessed Waters, practically makes a cross with his finger to protect himself from me, the devil's servant. Laurence, the secretary—we're on a first-name basis now, everybody calls me by my first name, I'm no prude—laughs, discreetly. Okay, so maybe she's not as uptight as I thought . . . She's even kind of checking me out.

"He's a defrocked priest."

I burst out laughing.

"Defrocked? He lost his frock?"

"No, just his cassock . . . he was with the Church but decided to go back to civilian life, if you will."

"You know, your boss isn't gonna have much fun with a guy like that, huh?"

"What makes you think he's going to keep you?"

In fact, the priest disappeared after eight days. He had warned the Pozzo against the Muslim devil he'd carelessly allowed into his home. Muslim, me? I'd never set foot in a mosque in my entire life. As for the devil, well . . . maybe a little still, but honestly: less and less, right?

25

One morning the transfer machine gets stuck. It's impossible to get it going. The Pozzo is already half in it, but only half. We'd slid the straps under his arms and thighs, he was dangling over the bed, not yet in the shower chair. You can imagine the level of comfort . . . So we had to call emergency services. By the time they got there and got him out, and followed the necessary process to get him in his chair, it was already the afternoon . . . That whole time, the Pozzo was polite, patient, and resigned, without looking defeated. We told all kinds of jokes to keep him distracted and play down the situation. Not because the machine was stuck: we knew it would start again sooner or later. But because a man was trapped in a device that was supposed to help him and he was helpless to get out of it. We send men to the moon and we're incapable of developing a faster, safer system for moving around a tetraplegic? The next morning, before even turning on the people-mover, I told the care assistant that I was going to carry Mr. Pozzo to his shower chair—me, Abdel Sellou, five feet, eight inches tall, with short, round arms like marshmallow sticks. She yelled at me.

"Are you crazy? This man is as fragile as an egg!"

His bones, lungs, skin: on a tetraplegic, every part of the body is vulnerable—injuries aren't visible to the eye, and pain doesn't sound the alarm. The blood doesn't circulate well, wounds don't heal, organs aren't well irrigated, the urinary and intestinal processes are affected, the body doesn't clean itself. Being around the Pozzo for a few days had provided me with accelerated medical training. I understood that he was a delicate patient. An egg, really. A quail's egg with a thin, white shell. I remember the state of my GI Joes after I played with them, when I was a kid. It wasn't pretty . . . But I was grown-up now. I looked at the Pozzo, a big GI Joe made of porcelain. The guy who'd been showing his nice, white teeth a few minutes earlier was now clenching them since I'd made the announcement that I'd carry him. But I was sure I could move the egg without breaking it.

"Monsieur Pozzo. I've been watching you for days now. This machine is a nightmare, and I think I've found a way to get around using it. Let me do it. I'll go very slowly."

"Are you sure, Abdel?"

"Listen, the worst thing is I hit a leg—you get a bedsore and that's it, right?"

"Well that's nothing, I can handle—"

"Okay, enough talk. Let's go."

I slipped my arms under his and pulled his chest against me—the rest of his body followed. He was sitting in his shower chair in hardly ten seconds. I looked at the result, pleased with myself, and yelled to the door, "Laurence! Bring me the toolkit! We're taking down the transfer machine!"

The Pozzo said nothing; he was smiling, thrilled.

"So, Monsieur Pozzo, who's the best?"

"You, Abdel, you!"

He smiled blissfully, with all of his white teeth. The moment had come to ask for an explanation.

"Monsieur Pozzo, tell me something, your teeth—are they real?"

26

I could have had business cards made. ABDEL SELLOU, SIMPLIFIER. Because in the whole we're-not-going-to-let-pain-in-the-ass-machines-ruin-our-lives process, I also got rid of the cattle wagon, a so-called ideal vehicle for transporting the handicapped. It was ugly, impractical, and, like the transfer machine, it broke down constantly.

The cattle wagon had a platform system that came out and lowered to allow the wheelchair to get in. It got stuck a lot. This was a problem when we needed to leave, because the Pozzo could miss his appointment, and on the way back, too, because the thing was too high for me to take the wheelchair—and the Pozzo in it—out by hand. Sometimes I had to get a plank and use it like a slide. In the cattle wagon, the Pozzo stayed seated in his usual spot, which was in the back on the right. The wheels weren't locked onto the floorboard and even if you pushed on the brakes, the wheelchair shifted around on turns. That was dangerous enough, even more so when the driver was named Sellou and had learned to drive on stolen cars in suburban parking lots . . . Plus, the Pozzo only had a tiny window and the engine made ridiculous noise. When I was at the wheel, I practically had to turn around in my seat to talk to the boss. So I didn't talk, I yelled.

"Are you okay? Not too bumpy?"

"Watch the road, Abdel!"

"What's that?"

"The road!"

I drove a Renault 25 GTS, thank you very much. Okay, these days it's kind of cheesy, but back then it was first-class. A car driven by guys who'd made it big. I bought it at auction in 1993, just after getting my license. It had been repossessed from some poor guy who couldn't keep up with the payments. As for me, the delinquent, the ex-con, I paid in cash. That's class . . . it had excellent pickup and a sweet stereo system. Worlds away from the cattle wagon.

I ended up going on strike. We were about to load up the Pozzo. I had my finger on the remote control for the platform, and I said no.

"What do you mean no, Abdel?"

"No, Monsieur Pozzo. No."

"No what?"

"No, I'm not driving this thing anymore. You're not a sheep, you know. You can get into a normal car."

"Unfortunately, Abdel, I can't."

"And you also couldn't do without the transfer machine, right? So. Don't move, I'm going to get my car."

"Trust me, Abdel, I'm not moving!"

I push the wheelchair to the handicapped spot where I'd parked my car equipped with a fake plate bearing a handicap symbol. That little sticker was great and definitely worth the *botte prioritaire* in the game Mille Bornes.

"Where did you get that sticker, Abdel?"

"It's a photocopy of the one on the cattle wagon. A laser color copy—it cost me a fortune!"

"Abdel, you can't do that, it isn't right . . ."

"It's so practical for parking in Paris. And it is right since I'm driving you in my car."

I open the passenger door, push the seat back as far as it will go, and park the wheelchair against the body of the car.

"What, you're not cheering for me? You cheer for Babette and not me?"

"Go, Abdel! Lift the Pozzo!"

Obviously, as I had just shown, you could get him into a normal car. We took off for Porte de la Chapelle. I knew that there we'd find some real gems on four wheels; this lover of beautiful things would find something he liked. I liked all cars.

When we looked at the cars there, I didn't say anything, just watched the Pozzo weaving around in his wheelchair between the Chrysler and the Rolls-Royce, the Rolls and the Porsche, the Porsche and the Lamborghini, the Lamborghini and the Ferrari . . .

"This one's not bad! The black is sober. What do you think, Abdel?"

"Monsieur Pozzo, the Ferrari's trunk might be a little too small."

"Did you plan on putting me in the trunk?"

"Not you, but the chair?"

"Oh shit! I forgot about that . . ."

He finally decided on a Jaguar XJS 3.6 liter, square headlights, walnut dashboard, leather interior . . . It was due to be sold by auction.

"Do you like it, Abdel?"

"Yeah, it'll do . . ."

"Shall we buy it?"

"We'll have to be patient, Monsieur Pozzo. The auction is in three days."

"Okay, we'll wait . . . but not a word to my wife, all right?"

"I swear. I'll be as quiet as a roach."

"As a mouse, Abdel, as a mouse."

"As a mouse, too, if you want!"

27

So now I drive the Pozzo or his wife, who just had a bone mar-
row transplant, to the hospital in a Jaguar. The operation's a
last chance: the doctors only give her four to six months to live.
Everything went well in the OR and in post-op, but it isn't over
yet. Her immune system is shot. She has to stay in a bubble in
a sterilized room.

Every morning for weeks, I take the Pozzo in the Jaguar
to go be next to her. As next to her as he can get: behind the
isolation curtain. With a hospital bonnet on his head and plastic socks over his Westons, he rolls up to the barrier you're not
supposed to cross. He watches his wife for hours, lying in her
bed, a little delirious. We leave her in the evening with the fear
that we won't find her in better condition the next morning.
And then, the verdict comes from the doctors' mouths.

Madame Pozzo is going to die.

I'm silent in the Jaguar.

No more nurse's assistants. No more nurses. I am now the last face Philippe Pozzo di Borgo sees at night and the first one he sees in the morning. Since that first time I carried him, we haven't really needed anybody. Now that his wife is dead, he is sleeping alone. He watched her go, unbelieving, crazy with rage. He'd only ever known her while she was sick and he'd loved her despite that, despite the everyday discomfort, even though he was in such good health and went off to the countryside every weekend, even though he flew over mountains. He'd had that terrible paragliding accident on June 23, 1993, and, for two years, his wife's illness had taken a backseat. Everyone thought it was a remission—that the treatments were finally working, that she'd live longer, why not? She'd found the strength to organize a new life for the whole family, built around her husband's handicap. They'd left their house in Champagne to come to Paris and its hospitals. They'd created a comfortable place to live for everyone—obviously, it's easier with money—and the kids seemed to adjust as much as possible to their new life in the capital, with a father in a wheelchair and a sick mother . . . And just when everything seemed to be in place, when all the obstacles to having an almost normal life had been removed, Béatrice Pozzo di Borgo had relapsed.

I'd been living with them for about a year when it happened. Madame Pozzo hadn't been consulted on the choice of life auxiliary, who wasn't really one. She didn't veto the choice when she saw this young, undereducated, and unpredictable Arab show up at her house. She observed me without judgment and accepted me right away. She laughed at my jokes without joining in, from a certain distance, but always with kindness. I know she was a little afraid sometimes when she saw me take off with her husband without telling her before and without saying where we were going. I know that she didn't approve of us buying a luxury car. It was her Protestant side: she never liked ostentatious signs of wealth. She was a simple woman, and I respected her. For the first time, I didn't judge a rich lady for being just that.

In one year, what had the Pozzo and I done? Just gotten to know each other. He'd tried to question me about my parents. I think he even wanted to meet them. I avoided the problem.

"You know, Abdel, it's important to be at peace with your family. Do you know your country, Algeria?"

"My country is right here and I'm at peace with myself."

"I'm not sure about that, Abdel."

"Okay, that's enough."

"That's enough, Abdel. We won't talk about it anymore . . ."

The cattle wagon wasn't cut out for rodeos on the beltway, but the Jaguar was. I was the one who stepped on the gas, but it was both of us who went over the limit. Just one word from him would have been enough to make me slow down. The Pozzo was watching his wife disappear, he didn't express his pain, he was watching the movie of his life as a spectator. I pushed a little harder on the pedal. He turned his head slightly toward me, the motor rumbled, I burst out laughing, hard, as hard as possible, he turned his head the other way. He was giving up. We were racing ahead, together, come what may.

One year was long enough for both of us to know, without saying it out loud, that I was going to stay. If I'd had to leave, I would have done it sooner. I wouldn't have said yes to the trip to Martinique, a few weeks before the transplant.

"This will be Béatrice's last vacation for a long while; let's all three go!" said the Pozzo to try to convince me.

I'd never been farther than Marseille, so there was no need to convince me of anything. The "last vacation for long while" argument was baloney; we all knew it. The last vacation, period . . . We knew the risk involved in Béatrice's bone marrow transplant. But it was her husband who got sick in Martinique. Pulmonary congestion: secretions accumulated in his bronchial tubes and he had a difficult time breathing. He was taken into intensive care and stayed there for the whole trip. I had one-on-one lunches with Béatrice at the beach. We didn't say much to each other. It wasn't necessary, but it wasn't uncomfortable, either. I wasn't the man she loved. I also wasn't the one she'd have liked to see sitting there, with two working arms, one bringing a fork to his mouth and the other crossing the table to take her hand. That man didn't exist anymore anyway; she had to give him up at the time of the paragliding accident, so she might as well be happy with this slightly heavy and poorly behaved, but not really dangerous guy.

I like to think she thought me capable of taking care of her husband through the challenges to come. I like to think that she trusted me. But maybe she didn't think any of that. Maybe she had also simply given up. When you're no longer controlling anything, that's got to be the only thing to do, right? Let go, at one hundred fifty miles an hour on the banks of the Seine or sitting comfortably in a paradisiacal setting, under the sun, facing the turquoise sea.

⌁

I didn't think he'd survive his wife's death. He didn't want to leave his bed for weeks. When family members visited, he barely looked at them. Céline took care of the kids—consoling and practical at the same time, she kept them at a distance, seeing they had enough on their plate with their own grief. I buzzed around the Pozzo constantly. But he didn't let me distract him anymore. Dignified even in his depression, he only asked to be presentable for medical visits. We'd gotten by without nursing assistants and nurses for months because he'd wanted to, and because he got a wicked pleasure out of showing people that he did just fine using only Abdel's arms and legs. We had to call them back, and they came immediately, competent and devoted. Monsieur Pozzo couldn't stand the idea of so many people fussing over his body, three-quarters dead, when nobody could do anything for his wife's.

Luckily, I was young and impatient. Luckily, I didn't understand anything. I said "enough."

IV

Learning to Live Differently

28

"*Monsieur Pozzo, that's enough, it's time to get up now!*"

"I want to be alone, Abdel. Leave now, please."

"You've been alone long enough. I've had it. You like it, you don't like it, it doesn't matter. We're getting dressed and we're going out . . . Plus, I know you're going to like this."

"Whatever you say . . ."

The Pozzo sighs. The Pozzo turns his head, looking for nothing, an empty space without hands moving in it, without any looks. He blocks out the moving mouths.

⌒

I don't want to call him the Pozzo anymore. He isn't a thing, an animal, a toy, a doll. The man in front of me is suffering and doesn't look anywhere except inside himself anymore, at his memories, at what isn't any longer, probably. I try my best to dart around devilishly, dance the cucaracha, play pranks on Laurence that make her scream, but he doesn't register any of it. What the hell am I doing here? He could ask me why I was still sticking around, because I wonder myself . . .

I'd give him a stupid answer.

I'd answer that I'm staying for the comfortable Louis-Philippe sofa in his room that I haven't left since Béatrice died. I'd sublet the top-floor apartment to a girlfriend. Nobody here knows about it. I'm being honest and I really like this girl, so I'm not asking much for rent. What? A thousand francs per month. That's way below market price.

I'd answer that I'm staying for the Jaguar. That I'd like him to pull himself together, a little, so that I could leave him at night and start up my nighttime drives again. That car is a magnet for women. Well, certain kinds of women . . . I know: I'm not going to find my Béatrice among the ones who get in for a ride. The ones who get in are the ones who are only interested in money. We don't know each other; we're not going to know each other. I let them know when it's over, always a bastard and proud of it.

"This car belongs to my boss. You want me to drop you off at the next metro station?"

I'd answer that I'm staying because I love going to eat the little samples of food they give you in expensive gourmet restaurants and then indulge in a Greek sandwich on my way out.

I'd answer that I'm staying because I still haven't seen *La Traviata* live and I'm counting on him to take me to the opera (he made me listen to some of it one day, explained the story to me, it bored me to death . . . I seriously thought I was going to die).

I'd answer that I'm staying because I want to have fun, because I'm alive, because life is for having fun and you can do that more easily when you have money to spend. It just so happens that he has some and he's alive, too, so that works out well!

I'd answer that I'm staying for his money. By the way, that's what most of his friends think: they don't all keep quiet. I hate disappointing overly confident people. They dig their feet into their certainties; it's quite a show.

He'd keep asking:

"Why are you staying, Abdel?"

I wouldn't answer that I'm staying for him, because we aren't all dogs, for God's sake.

I dress him in his light gray Cerruti suit, a blue shirt, gold cufflinks, and a tie with blood-red stripes. A drop of Eau Sauvage, his cologne for the last thirty years—the same as his father. I brush his hair and smooth his mustache.

"Where are you taking me Abdel?

"To get oysters? Would you like to eat some oysters? I'm craving oysters, personally . . ."

I lick my lips and rub my belly. He smiles. He knows I hate oysters, especially during summer, when they're all milky. But he loves them with a little lemon juice or some shallot sauce. We're going to Normandy.

"Shall we take a CD in the car? What do you want to listen to, Monsieur Pozzo?"

"Gustav Mahler."

I put two fingers sideways under my nose like a Hitler mustache, put on a German accent, and get angry.

"Goustaf Mahluh? Ach nein, Meestah Pozzo! Zatz enough now! Enough!"

He hints at a smile. That's a start . . .

⌐

The Jaguar is a beautiful but dangerous car. You can't feel the speed. It flies, we levitate, we don't feel anything. On the way to Raymond Poincaré Hospital in Garches, I hadn't noticed that it rears like a horse about to gallop.

We are all set, Monsieur Pozzo and me, listening to France Musique, a nice little symphony like the one you get on the phone when you call the social security office. Two motorcycle cops catch up to us on the Saint-Cloud bridge. I see them in the rearview mirror and glance at the speedometer: eighty miles per hour . . . Monsieur Pozzo's in good shape today, so I give it a try.

"There's two cops there, going to stop us soon."

"Oh . . . Abdel! We're going to be late."

"Well, yes, we definitely will be, Monsieur Pozzo. Don't you want to try using your bad-day face?"

The police are getting dangerously close.

"What's my bad-day face?"

I make a face like I'm horribly constipated, and he bursts out laughing.

"No, now, Monsieur Pozzo, you can't laugh right now, you have to suffer! Come on, I'm counting on you!"

I slow down significantly, put my signal on, and start to pull over to the shoulder. I lower the window.

"Abdel!"

"Three, two, one . . . Suffer!"

I don't look at them, I'm afraid of cracking up. I lean toward the cop who's approaching carefully. I play the dumb guy who's completely freaking out.

"He's having an attack! It's my boss. He's a tetraplegic. He's having a heart attack, I'm taking him to Garches, we don't have time to stop, he's gonna die!"

"Turn off the engine, sir."

I obey, with difficulty. I punch the steering wheel.

"I'm telling you, we don't have time!"

The other policeman comes up. He walks around the car, suspicious, and addresses my passenger.

"Sir, lower your window, please. Sir, sir!"

"How's he supposed to lower the window? You know what tetraplegic means? Te-tra-ple-gic!"

"He's paralyzed?"

"Hooray, he gets it!"

They both look at me: they're angry because of the tone I'm using, worried not to be in control of the situation, and annoyed. I risk glancing at Monsieur Pozzo. He's fantastic. He's let his head droop to his shoulder, his forehead stuck to the door, his eyes are rolling and on top of it he's moooaanning . . . He doesn't look at all like he does on bad days, but I'm the only one to know it.

"Listen," says the first one, nervous, "where are you going in such a hurry?"

"To the Raymond Poincaré Hospital in Garches, I told you! It's urgent!"

"I'll call an ambulance right now."

"Oh, no, it'll take too long, he won't make it! This is what we're going to do: you know the way to Garches? Yes? Great!

So get in front of us and your colleague can get behind us. Let's go!"

I start the engine and step on the gas to show my determination. After a second's hesitation—because policeman often hesitate by nature—the guys put on their helmets and arrange themselves like I told them. We head to the hospital, at a moderate speed; the cops hold their bikes with one hand and gesture for cars to move aside with the other.

Monsieur Pozzo lifts his head a little and asks me, "And what's your plan when we get there, Abdel?"

"Well, we do what we said! Aren't you supposed to host a conference for the handicapped?"

"Yes, yes . . ."

In the hospital parking lot, I quickly unload Monsieur Pozzo's folding wheelchair, open the passenger side door, carry the favorite for the Oscar for Best Actor and bluntly cut off one of the motorcycle cops who offered help.

"Absolutely not, my friend. This man is as fragile as an egg!"

"Ahhhh," said the dying man.

I pushed him toward the ER entrance at a jog while yelling back to the cops: "It's okay now, you can go! If he doesn't die, I won't file a complaint against you!"

We waited for them to leave before walking back out: we weren't in the right place for the conference. The boss was laughing harder than he'd laughed in weeks.

"So, who's the best?"

"You, Abdel, it's still you!"

"Hey, hey . . . you, on the other hand, you didn't look like you were having an attack at all! What was that face?"

"Abdel, have you ever seen *La Traviata*?"

"Haven't seen it, no. But thanks to you, I know the story, thank you very much."

"I was doing Violetta, at the end . . ."

And he sings.

"Gran Dio! Morir si giovine . . ."

29

You count time for tetraplegics like you do for dogs: one year of life is actually equal to seven. Philippe Pozzo di Borgo had his accident three years earlier at the age of forty-two. Three times seven equals twenty-one added on: so in 1996, you could say that he was sixty-three years old. Still, he didn't look like Agécanonix, the really old guy in the Astérix comic, all small, all shriveled, his heart as dry as his hair . . . The count had the look of a lord and the spirit of a twenty-year-old.

"Monsieur Pozzo, you need a woman."

"A woman, Abdel? Mine is dead, remember?"

"We're going to find another. Okay, it won't be the same, but it'll be better than nothing."

"But what would I do to the poor thing?"

"You'll talk to her sweetly, like Cyrano de Bergerac to Roxanne."

"Bravo Abdel! I see my literature lessons are bearing fruit!"

"You'll teach me to read, I'll teach you to live."

I invite friends to come over. Aïcha, a small brunette with a large bust, both beautiful and a nurse at the same time, understood the situation. During her first visit, we all had a drink together. The next day, I left early. The day after that, she lay down on the bed. For a while, Monsieur Pozzo and she slept in the bed together. Aïcha didn't want money or presents. She was interested in this man who could speak so well, but she wasn't a gold digger . . . He had no illusions: he wasn't going to fall in love with her, nor she with him, but they had some nice times together. Aïcha breathed calmly, he felt her breath, the warmth of her body, she calmed him. There were a few others afterward, professional companions, happy to work and have a rest at the same time.

I warned them: "You have to be gentle with my boss, and talk politely. Spit out your chewing gum before you come here and watch your language—no talking like a truck driver!"

Monsieur Pozzo slowly got over the death of his wife. Very slowly . . . Sometimes I caught him staring into space, a disembodied soul, the spectator entirely disconnected from the joys of life, and hopeless to someday share in them. Despite Aïcha and the heady scents of his temporary companions, he wasn't really any better. Béatrice had been gone for several months, Laurence was on vacation, the kids were withering in Paris. I suggested a little trip.

"Monsieur Pozzo, don't you have a little place in the South?"

"A little place . . . no, I don't know what you . . . Oh, yes, there's La Punta in Corsica. Our family sold it to the departmental council a few years ago but the tower is still ours to use, next to the family vault."

"In a cemetery, that sounds like fun . . . Is that all you've got to offer?"

"That's all, yes."

"Well, let's do it! I'll pack the bags."

There are eight of us packed into the cattle wagon (it had to be done: we couldn't all fit into the Jaguar). Céline and the kids are coming along, of course, but there's also Victor, Monsieur Pozzo's nephew; his sister Sandra; and her son, Théo. It's hot, but not hot enough yet. We only turn on the AC from time to time and nobody complains. A tetraplegic is always cold. We cover him with blankets, hats, wool, it's never enough. I saw a lot of them in Kerpape, at Morbihan, the physical rehabilitation center where Monsieur Pozzo normally goes for his annual checkup. At first light, the wheelchairs line up in front of the south-facing window and stay there. In the wagon, Philippe Pozzo di Borgo puts on a brave face for his kids. I know he's still mourning his wife, that he hates all of us all a little for being there when she isn't. We sweat, our odors mix, but at least he isn't cold.

We cover the miles without speeding. Each of us takes a turn sighing, except for me. Céline just opens an eye and stretches.

"Look, we're at Montélimar . . . can we stop and get some nougat?"

I grumble that if we start pulling over every time a culinary specialty becomes available, we'll never get there . . .

She doesn't say anything, I think she's pouting a little. And then:

"Abdel, is that smoke normal?"

I look on either side of the highway, I don't see anything.

"Did you see a forest fire or something?"

"No, I'm talking about the smoke pouring out of the hood. That's strange, right?"

It's bad even. The engine's dead. I had wanted to get rid of the cattle wagon once and for all—well, now it's done. It sits immobilized in the emergency lane. I'm alone with four children, two women and a tetraplegic in August. It's now 104 degrees in the shade, and there are still 120 miles to Marseille, where we're supposed to set sail for Corsica in less than four hours, everything's fine . . . They're all laughing at me, lighthearted, grinning. I forgot to check the oil. Or the water. Or both—what do I know? I keep cool.

"There's got to be car insurance papers somewhere in the doors, right? Yes, here it is! Ha, you're going to love this: it's only valid for another week. Lucky we didn't break down on the way back, huh?"

The boss is cracking up.

I take out my mobile phone, an accessory already available to the greater population at that time, and start by calling a tow truck. Then I try rental car companies. In vain. The summer's in full swing, there are tourists in Montélimar like there are everywhere else, we're not going to find anything. I contact the carmaker's customer service. I scream into the telephone saying it's inadmissible to leave a tetraplegic on the side of the road. I use my famous line, still the same, regarding my very special passenger:

"He's a tetraplegic, you know what that means? Te-tra-ple-gic!"

Everyone's laughing back in the car, which is still exhaling a stream of black smoke.

"Abdel, why are you getting angry? Aren't we lucky to be here on the road in the land of nougat?"

Customer service offers us a refund for the cost of the trip from Montélimar to Marseille by taxi. But we're on our own for getting to Montélimar. Just then, the tow truck arrives. Everybody on board! The mechanic, a guy in his sixties who seems to have had way too much of the local specialty given the size of his waist, expresses his displeasure with a chipper tone.

"Oh no, I can only take two or three people in the truck. And anyway, you just can't do that."

"We're going to stay in the cattle wagon."

"Oh, no, that's against the rules, sir. You can't do that."

I drag him by the collar all the way to the sliding door on the wagon and show him the wheelchair.

"You want me to push him for fifteen miles in the emergency lane?"

"Oh, no, you're right sir. You can't do that, either."

"Okay, I can't do that . . . so let's load up!"

Alexandra, Victor, and Théo climb into the driver's side of the tow truck while he takes care of getting the cattle wagon onto the platform. We haven't gotten Monsieur Pozzo out. Laetitia, Robert-Jean, Céline, and I try to hold his chair upright during the maneuver. We pitch hard . . . the kids are splitting their sides. They imitate the mechanic's accent: "You can't do that, you can't do that!" That will be the theme for this vacation. I think I catch Philippe Pozzo di Borgo laughing, too, and genuinely.

We get to the port of Marseille. Just in time: the boat's leaving in twenty minutes. Theoretically . . . I've paid for the two cabs and, just when they leave, Céline starts to worry.

"For a huge vacation departure day, there don't seem to be many people, right? Did everyone board already? The boat looks empty . . ."

It's true—the white and yellow cruise ship looks completely abandoned. There's no one on the dock besides us and the vehicle ramp is raised . . . I run to go ask the port authority. I get back to our little group that's found a shady spot in the also deserted port.

"You're gonna laugh—the port authority's closed."

"Really? There's nothing written anywhere?"

"Oh yes, there is . . . it says the shipping company's on strike, indefinitely."

Nobody says a word for several seconds. Until Victor's little voice justly pipes up: "You can't do that!"

I got more information on the telephone from the company that sold us the tickets for the boat. They were suggesting we go to Toulon, where we'd be able to make the crossing. Toulon, more than forty miles away . . . I tried calling a taxi. Nothing doing. So I took off on foot, alone, to the Marseille train station, to get not one, but two taxis. The train travelers were trying to get cabs, too. No taxis. I headed back toward the center of town, went down the smaller streets leading to the Casbah d'Alger. I spoke in Arabic to the old men chewing tobacco on the doorsteps and ended up finding one ready to help us out in exchange for a small bill.

~

The look on the others' faces when they saw us drive up to the port . . . Our chauffeur was the lucky owner of a Peugeot 305 wagon so run-down that he wasn't allowed to leave the country that summer.

"Abdel, we're not really going to get in that thing, are we?"

"But of course we are, dear Laetitia! Unless you prefer to stay here?"

"You're seriously crazy! I'm not getting in, I'm not getting in!"

The teen, spoiled to the tips of her toes—manicured of course, she's fifteen!—has a giant tantrum. She's absolutely horrified. Her father reacts, incredulous: "Abdel, comfort aside, how do you expect eight of us to get in that?"

"Nine, of us, Monsieur Pozzo, nine! You're forgetting the driver . . ."

But we did it. Even Laetitia survived.

30

This kind of scene always gets laughs in the movies ... Well ... the audience laughs, not the characters. When things get tough, old accounts are settled, little minor wrongdoings come back up, people's true natures are revealed. They could have turned on me, all of them, and judged me as responsible for the break-down since I was the driver, come down on me hard because I let the two taxis leave too soon, because there weren't enough bottles of water in the wagon, because it was me, after all, who had the idea for this vacation! But not one of them made the slightest negative remark. Just like in the cattle wagon when they all put up with the heat without complaining, they decided to see the humor in the situation. For their father, their brother, their uncle, who didn't complain. For Monsieur Pozzo, the first one to laugh at the absurdity of our bad luck. The trip from Paris to Marseille had exhausted him, much more so than us; he had even endured being shaken and been subjected to the noise of the cattle wagon and our chatter. He blamed sheer fatigue, but he had put his already fragile health in danger. Still, he didn't complain. He looked at us, one after the other, as if he were rediscovering new joy in being alive and one of us. I don't just mean one of the members of his family; I mean one of us.

I ended up at his side by accident less than a year before and stayed there almost without even deciding to. Against all odds, I acted like a real assistant: I had turned the pages of his newspaper, put in the disc he wanted to listen to, took him to the café when he wanted, mixed the sugar into his beverage and held the cup to his lips. Through my body, everything I could do, by my strength and my joy for living, I made up for his handicap. During the weeks before Béatrice's death, and the few weeks after, I didn't leave him for an instant. The word *job* didn't mean the same thing to me as it does to a guy who's afraid of losing his and not being able to pay his bills. I didn't care about job security and I was still insolent enough to leave at the drop of a hat if I felt like it. There were no hours; I had no more private life. I didn't even see my friends and I didn't care. Why did I stay? I wasn't a hero or a nun. I stayed because we aren't just animals . . .

I got through those difficult hours by respecting the same logic as I did at Fleury-Mérogis: the situation was bad, I wasn't in control of it, but I knew it wasn't permanent. I just had to wait it out. Weeks later, in the Marseille harbor, facing a cruise ship with no one waiting for us, I realized I was free again because Monsieur Pozzo, stuck in an absurd situation once again, was choosing life.

So, looking at this man who had the gift of laughter, I understood that something other than the job connected us. It had nothing to do with a contract or a moral obligation. I was hiding something from my friends and even from my parents that I wasn't even aware of: I assured them I was staying with my boss to take advantage of his generous gifts, to travel with him, to enjoy the comforts of plush furniture and drive around in a sports car. There was a little of that, for sure, but so little. I really believe I loved this man, as simple as that, and that he returned the affection just as naturally.

But I'd rather die in a paragliding accident than admit it.

31

I go everywhere with Monsieur Pozzo. Absolutely everywhere.
Now that he's—sort of—gotten over his wife's death, we man-
age again without the help of nurses and nurse's aids. I've
learned what needs to be done, treating the bedsores, trimming
away the pieces of dead flesh, putting in the catheter. I'm not
disgusted. We're all made the same way. It's understanding the
pain that took me a long time. I never got a laugh from emp-
tying a hot teapot onto his legs like my character does in the
film *Intouchables:* Monsieur Pozzo doesn't feel anything, sure,
I get it. So why does he scream like that? He's sensitive to what
doesn't work normally inside his body. Something to do with
nerve endings, apparently. The only thing linking his soul to its
envelope comes from this pain, never from pleasure. What luck
. . .

We finally got to Corsica. I was expecting to stay in one of those rich people's homes that see you around there, like with old stone and an infinity pool, and here I am in the ruins of a chateau in the mountains just near Ajaccio. The history of the place is fascinating. The chateau was built with the remains of a palace that had stood in the Tuileries and was burned by the Communards— a new generation of revolutionaries, if I understood correctly— in 1871. A dozen years later, when it was about to be completely demolished, Pozzo's grandfather bought the stones, had them transported to Corsica, and had them used to build an identical structure. When I see the way things work today . . . They've started restoring the roof. There don't seem to be too many workers and they're going to be at it for at least ten years.

We stay in a nearby tower that we have to cross a suspension bridge to get to—it's the Middle Ages. I joke with Monsieur Pozzo, calling him Godefroy de Montmirail. He didn't see *Les Visiteurs;* I don't think French comedies are his thing.

His ancestors are laid to rest in a chapel a few hundred feet away. Monsieur Pozzo tells me that he has a spot waiting for him. Let it wait . . . He gets really sick—exhausted from the chaotic journey, no doubt. A vesicle blockage that seems impossible to cure. For three days and three nights, I see him suffer like never before. At the work site, the men hit with their hammers. They stop now and then, surprised by the intensity of the screams coming from the tower. Seriously, I've never seen a man cry that much.

"Don't you think we should go to the hospital?"

"No Abdel, please, I want to stay at home. I don't want to miss the party."

We'd planned to invite the people over from the village next to the chateau. They had mourned Lady Béatrice three months earlier and the count intends to thank them. But he's stuck in bed and no painkiller has any effect. He can only get relief at the hospital. He doesn't want to go, and I give in. The kids feel right at home at La Punta; they have memories of coming here as a family. Monsieur Pozzo remembers Béatrice in this place full of history and their history, and I can't see myself depriving them of this rediscovery.

It seems like I did the right thing. On the morning of the party, the pain goes away. We organize a North African–style barbecue. I go get the sheep, slaughter it, and roast it like a servant from another era. The members of the polyphonic choir Alata have come. They sing in a circle, each turned toward the next one, with a hand over an ear. Their deep voices resonate in the trees and bushes. You'd have to be a fool not to appreciate it. It even does something to me . . . The party is fantastic, the lord reigns from his wheelchair, delivered from physical pain and from the slightest hint of his sadness.

We're always together.

I take Monsieur Pozzo to the doctors at Kerpape, the physical rehabilitation center in Brittany where he was treated after his accident. He announces to the staff, jovially, "Let Dr. Abdel through."

He's a grateful man.

I go with Monsieur Pozzo to his dinner invitations. In restaurants, I move the chairs and tables, I arrange the cutlery so that I can feed him neatly. Sometimes, they forget to feed the care assistant—me. Monsieur Pozzo politely tells the head-waiter that I eat, too.

One Sunday, we're eating with one of the most traditional families. The kids are wearing navy suits with white shirts, the girls in pleated skirts and Peter Pan collars. They say some kind of prayer before digging in. I burst out laughing. I quietly say, "It's like the Ingalls family!"

Monsieur Pozzo looks at me, panicked.

"Abdel, get a hold of yourself. And who is the Ingalls family, anyway?"

"We need to work on your culture! They're the people on *Little House on the Prairie*!"

Everybody at the table's heard me. They stare at me, furious. Monsieur Pozzo has the kindness not to apologize for me.

I go with him to dinner organized by people from his world. They don't know too many Arabs, except maybe for their cleaning ladies. They ask me questions about my life, my plans, my ambitions.

"Ambitions? I don't have any."

"Come now, Abdel, you seem intelligent and hardworking. You could certainly do something."

"I take advantage. It's not bad, taking advantage. You should all try it sometime. You'd look a lot better!"

On the way back, Monsieur Pozzo lectures me.

"Abdel, thanks to you they're going to think all Arabs are lazy and they're going to vote for the Nationalist party."

"You think they waited until they knew me to do that?"

~

It's the opening of the International Contemporary Art Fair, or ICAF. The boss, an occasional collector, is invited to the preshow for several galleries: the opening without the crowd. Just us folks, right . . . These people are stinking rich and reek of disdain. And most of all, what a bunch of snobs . . . Three square feet of thick carpet placed on the ground right in the middle of a booth. Hey, a red doormat! But what's it for? Wait a minute, there's a little tag next to it. It's the instruction manual: you're not supposed to walk on it, just drag your hand over it. And the work is complete until another hand transforms it or erases it. Bullshit. I'm bent over, but not to be the artist. I'm counting the zeros, lined up closely in small characters on the card. We're in the hundreds of thousands of dollars. You've got to be kidding me!

"Do you like it, Abdel?"

Monsieur Pozzo has seen my surprise and is having a laugh.

"Honestly, I'll take you to Home Depot and buy you the same thing for five francs! And you can even pick the color!"

We continue our little tour of the rip-off artists. A ball of blue wool levitates on the top of a rod. Is that for dusting in corners? An old slide projector clicks noisily every five seconds, displaying on the wall a black-and-white picture of a beach. That's art? The photos are all bad, you can't even see the girls' breasts! Lines of every color intersect on a canvas. There are also some triangles here and there, all kinds of shapes, scribbling . . . I'm trying to find something clear, a subject, an animal, a character, a house, a planet . . . I tilt my head in every direction; I lean forward and I look upside down through my legs. Even in that position, I don't see anything.

"It's lyrical abstract art, Abdel."

"Lyrical like music?"

"Like music!"

"Yeah. It does exactly the same thing to me! Nothing! And how much does this thing cost? Ooh, la la! Even you can't afford this, and that's saying something!"

"Yes, I can."

"Yeah, but, you don't want to, right? You don't want to? I'm warning you, Monsieur Pozzo, don't count on me for putting the nail in the wall so that thing can hang in our faces all day!"

No, he doesn't want to. He keeps his money for dressers. Because they have auctions for dressers, too. Where does he get this obsession for collecting dressers? He doesn't even know what to put in the drawers. Doesn't matter, he has to buy dressers . . . it's true that in a thirty-five-hundred-square-foot apartment, they fill the wall space. He finds them in auction catalogs from Drouot and others and, when he's not feeling up to it, sends me in his place. Usually he regrets it: I always get the object, but I go over the authorized maximum amount. He sighs and kicks himself for his excessive confidence. I pretend to be the passionate buyer.

"But Monsieur Pozzo, I couldn't let this one get away! I loved it too much!"

"Do you want to have it installed in your room, Abdel?"

"Uh, well, no . . . that's really nice, but it'd be a shame to take it away from you."

32

I got arrested at the wheel of the Jaguar. I wasn't even speed-
ing, I hadn't run any lights. Two undercover cops pinned me on
the sidewalk, flashing lights on, siren wailing. They saw a
poorly shaved, poorly dressed North African in a luxury car
and didn't ask any more questions. I ended up lying face down
on the hood without having had any time to explain myself.

"Easy, you're going to scratch the paint . . . it's my boss's
car."

They laugh behind me.

"And what've you got a boss for?"

"I'm a driver and life assistant. He's tetraplegic. You know
what that means—tetraplegic? Te-tra-ple-gic! Call him if you
want! His name is Philippe Pozzo di Borgo, he lives in the
XVIth, avenue Léopold II. The telephone number's on the
insurance contract in the side of the door."

They sit me up, but I still have my hands cuffed behind my

back and their hateful eyes on me. After checking, they let me go and throw the car papers in my face.

Monsieur Pozzo got a kick out of my story the next day.

"So, Ayrton-Abdel, I was woken up by the police last night! Were they at least nice to you?"

"Angels!"

I wrecked the Jaguar. I said it before, that car is dangerous: you don't notice the speed. I didn't realize I was going too fast to take a curve at Porte d'Orléans. I spent the night in the X-ray department of the ER and the car went straight to the scrap yard. I went home with my tail between my legs.

"So, Ayrton-Abdel, I got woken up by the police again last night . . ."

I handed the keys to Monsieur Pozzo.

"I'm sorry, that's all that's left."

"Are you all right?"

I go with Monsieur Pozzo to a new luxury car auction: after all, we have to replace the Jaguar that I totaled. We've decided to take a navy blue Rolls-Royce Silver Spirit—so chic, with 240 horsepower, beige leather interior, and a dashboard in exotic wood. When you start the engine, the brand logo shows up by magic. It's like a winged mermaid. At the start of the auction, I raise my own hand. Then the auctioneer figures it out and watches for nods from Monsieur Pozzo. It takes two days to settle the paperwork. I get a friend to drop me off at Porte de la Chapelle and then go back to avenue Léopold II at the wheel of this beauty.

We're going for a drive right away. We take the banks of the Seine, we race to the frontier of Normandy, amazed by the silence in the car no matter how fast we're going.

"It's nice, isn't it, Abdel?"

"Oh, it's nice, there's nothing nicer."

"You'll be careful, right?"

"Of course!"

That night, at the foot of the Beaugrenelle projects, one of my friends questions my employer's mental health.

"He's nuts to let you drive that thing!"

I take everybody for a ride, one after the other, just like a ride at an amusement park.

"These things aren't for people like us!"

I say I don't know what that means—people like us. And I add that I don't know why it shouldn't be for me, Abdel Sellou. She cracks up.

"That's true, Abdel, but you're not like us!"

She's right. I only think about myself, I use people, I show off, I use women to have fun, I scare rich people, I look down on my brother, but I love my life with Pozzo. I play with Philippe Pozzo di Borgo like a kid plays with his parents: I try things, I always push the envelope a little further, I look for limits, I don't find them, I keep pushing. I'm so sure of myself, so full of myself, that I don't even realize he's changing me, without me even noticing.

33

Céline's left us. She's thinking about having children. She doesn't see herself being a cook all her life for teenagers who don't like anything anyway, a tetraplegic eternally on a special diet, and a guy addicted to gyro sandwiches. Good-bye, Céline. I cook for a few days. Everything goes smoothly. Except that three cleaning ladies quit one after the other, tired of cleaning up after me morning, noon and night . . . We welcome Jerry, a Filipino recommended by an employment agency. We should have banned him from the washing machine. He took it upon himself to wash all the boss' suits at 100 degrees. The result isn't pretty. Stoic in a three-piece Dior, the last one he's got left, Monsieur Pozzo takes in the rags that the young man hung back in his closet as if nothing were wrong.

"Abdel, you know that plaster cast by Giacometti in the living room, you know, the one next to the library? We can put the Hugo Boss jacket on him, I think it'll fit now . . ."

"Come on, Monsieur Pozzo, it's okay. Where we're going, all you'll need is a big wool cap."

~

We go on a trip. Aunt Eliane, a soft, petite woman ever present since Béatrice's death, is counting on putting her courageous Philippe in the good care of a congregation of Québécoise nuns. She's in cahoots with cousin Antoine who spends heavily on religious souvenirs. Both of them sold us the idea with a solid argument: they talked about "love therapy."

"Monsieur Pozzo! Love therapy! I've always said that's exactly what you need!"

"Abdel, we're not talking really talking about the same thing . . ."

Personally, I loved the idea right away. As usual, I only heard what I wanted to hear: everything about the monastery, the retreat, the seminary, and the Capuchin nuns escaped me. For me, Quebec is just an extension of America where people have the good taste to speak French. I can already see myself settling into the modernity, the big open spaces, surrounded by Betty Boop, Marilyn, and extra-large helpings of fries. And since they're promising love on top of it all . . . Laurence, Philippe Pozzo's faithful secretary, has invited herself: she's very into spirituality, meditation, all that crap. She wants to "make penance," she says. Penance for what? I always thought that girl was a little masochistic. Nice, but masochistic.

~

We land in Montréal, but we don't go straight to the nuns. It'd be a shame if we didn't have a look around first, right? I love the restaurants here. All-you-can-eat buffets everywhere! So as not to look like a pig by going back for multiple helpings, I bring the buffet trays straight to our table. But Monsieur Pozzo still hasn't given up on teaching me manners.

"Abdel, we don't do that . . . and you've been gaining weight lately, too, haven't you?"

"All muscle! Not everybody can say that."

"Touché, Abdel, touché . . ."

"Oh no, Monsieur Pozzo! I was talking about Laurence!"

To get around, we've rented a superb beige Pontiac. Superb, but not rare: here everybody's got the same one. It doesn't matter, I'm living my American dream, even if it's in Canada.

On the way to the monastery, the boss asks me to stop and buy him cigarettes. He's afraid he won't be able to get any once we're there. He's kind of worrying me.

"If you run out, I'll go buy you some, don't worry!"

"Abdel, once we're there, we don't go anywhere. We adjust ourselves to the Capuchin rhythm and follow the seminary program until it's finished. Till the end of the week."

"Program? What program? And what? We don't leave the hotel for eight days?"

"Not the hotel, no, the monastery . . ."

"Yeah, but it's kind of the same, right? So, how many packs?"

I park the Pontiac in front of the drugstore window. I go buy his drug and come back to the car. I open the driver's side door and drop into my seat. I turn my head and expect to see my boss, as usual. But he's changed color, as well as gender. There's an enormous black woman sitting there.

"What did you do with the little white tadpole sitting here a minute ago?"

She looks at me, raising her eyebrows up to the roots of her braids.

"Are you kidding me? And who are you, first of all?"

I look in the rearview mirror. In the Pontiac parked just behind us sits Monsieur Pozzo, hysterical, and I imagine Laurence is laid out on the backseat, dying from laughter, may God have her soul.

Suddenly, I feel like a complete idiot.

"I'm sorry, ma'am. Really, uh, really sorry. I didn't mean to scare you."

"I'm not scared of you at all, little white man!"

White man! She called me white man! It took crossing the Atlantic to get called a white man!

I go back to the car, tail between my legs. It's true—she didn't look so terrified . . . It's also true that I must weigh a hundred pounds less than she does. And apparently I'm gaining weight. I've got some room to grow!

The monastery looks like a chalet in the Savoy region: wood everywhere, no bars on the windows, a lake, boats. Do these ladies supply fishing rods? Philippe Pozzo is one of the very special guests: usually, the nuns only open their home to women. Like at school in the old days: girls on one side, boys on the other. No mixing! But a tetraplegic, that's different . . . The boss has been cruelly deprived of his virility ever since his accident, but I think it's too blunt to remind him that he can't mix like before. As for me, I'm admitted as an "auxiliary." I still like that word as much as ever. I've had the time to think about what meaning to give it: like in grammar, the auxiliary has no use by itself. You have to put it with a verb or it's worthless. As with *I have*, for example. I have what? I have driven. I have eaten. I have slept. There, okay. I'm the auxiliary and Monsieur Pozzo is the verb. He's the one who drives, eats, sleeps. But without me, he can't. But what the nuns don't know is that Abdel the auxiliary has special autonomy in the grammar of life. They'll find out soon.

They give me a room on the ground floor, right next to my boss's room—no, you can't make me admit that it's called a cell. The car is parked in the lot. I'm relaxed: tonight, my verb is "to sleep." As soon as I've put Monsieur Pozzo to bed, I'm planning to sneak out through the window and drive to the nearest town. In the meantime, I play along. I observe, just like I always do when I get to a new place I don't know. I put my employer's wheelchair at the edge of the aisle in the church. I park myself against a pillar close by and snooze with one eye open. The seminary attendees all look a little broken down, either physically or emotionally, or both. They're focused on their suffering; they don't let go of it; they absorb it and try to detach themselves from it through prayer. I don't feel like a part of this. Some are stuck in wheelchairs, like Monsieur Pozzo. I watch them: I'm absolutely certain that if the employment agency had sent me to them, I wouldn't have stayed. They look so unhappy! All the fuses have blown, all the lightbulbs are out up there. With Pozzo, it's blinking. This guy look nothing like them. He's a warrior philosopher, a renegade Jedi from *Star Wars* . . . the Force is with him.

At the restaurant—no, I wouldn't call that place a dining hall—nobody talks. We chew and pray at the same time, that's the rule. Are we allowed to pray and ask that what we're eating taste better? When I think of the buffet restaurant just twenty minutes from here . . . Monsieur Pozzo and I have decided not to meet eyes. Definitely not! We burst out laughing right away. He can read my thoughts, and I can read his. We're not really absorbed in our meditations, he no more than I. A nun looks at me out of the corner of her eye. She has a look that would curl your hair, but if she isn't nice, I'm taking her in the Pontiac for a wild night in the Quebec countryside.

Except, I can't get out of the room by the window. It isn't locked, there aren't any bars, but the emergency escape ladder lands just in front of it on the outside. If the place goes up in flames, there'll be one fatality, just one. They'll pray for his soul, they'll call him Saint Abdel . . . I'm stuck. There isn't the slightest noise, we're lost in the sticks of Quebec, an owl hoots, a Capuchin snores, the emergency ladder is securely fastened to the wall, there's nothing to do. I'm going to bed.

The next day, I wink at the nun when we meet up in the hallway. She answers us directly:

"Hi! Is it true you've come from France?"

This creature is one of the faithful. She's used to these kinds of seminaries. She calls the local nuns by their first names. If she lets herself talk this loudly, it may be because she knows the real rules. I thought talking was banned.

"Yep, yes, we're Parisians . . . Hey, the talking rule is strict here!"

"Oh, well, come and sit with me tonight and we'll get to know each other . . ."

From three—Monsieur Pozzo, Laurence, and me—our group of whisperers has expanded to four. Then five, seven seminary attendees. Then ten, fifteen, twenty by the middle of the week. We weren't whispering anymore, and there was loud laughter at our table. The faces on which I'd seen the most pain when we arrived suddenly seemed more relaxed. Only one group of die-hard depressives stuck together at the end of the week. I called them party poopers. The Capuchins, who weren't even really trying to quiet us down, were laughing like hyenas.

"Ladies, you're going to have to rename your retreat."

"What do you mean, Abdel? You don't like 'Therapy Through Love'?"

"I think that 'Therapy Through Laughs' is a lot more effective."

34

Monsieur Pozzo gives stunning conferences to students from
the top business schools on a regular basis, and I go with him.
He talks to them about "capitalist brutality," the "subjugation
or exclusion of employees," the "financial crises against which
governments are powerless and that are pushing employees
toward more misery." He addresses the students listening to
him using *tu*—the informal pronoun for "you"—to reach each
and every of them. I've wedged his wheelchair against the
podium facing the white twenty-somethings dressed in suits
and ties. I've seated myself in a chair close to the side, head leaning against the wall. I'm not listening. He's boring me. I doze.
But every now and then, a power phrase, pronounced with even
more conviction than the others, wakes me up.

"Ethics are your ethics and action is your action. It's inside
of you, in your inwardness, in your mystery, in its silence that
you'll find the Other and the ground of your morals."

I think to myself that he does seem to know what he's talking about. About the silence, the inwardness. The Other. I'm one. Before his accident, when he was all-powerful, when he took baths in Pommery champagne like my mother does in peanut oil, would he have just looked at me? If I invited myself to a party thrown by his annoying daughter, I definitely would have left with the laptop. Today, when she invites little shits of her kind over, I provide the security.

The great, immobile sage, soul floating above his miserable carnal envelope, superior being delivered from flesh and earthly needs, keeps on going.

"It's when you've found that Other that your perspective and your action will align themselves."

Does he seriously believe this stuff? The kids sitting in front of him can already think of nothing other than eating each other alive, classmates or sons of the upper crust alike! All the big bosses would have to crash their paragliders to "find the Other" and respect people for who they are . . .

Okay, maybe guys like me would also have to stop doing stupid things. Like Monsieur Pozzo says, to the group of words "solidarity," "serenity," "fraternity," and "respect" we need to add "humility." I hear what he's saying, but I'm the best. It's tested, proven, confirmed by the boss ten times a day. So as for humility . . . I go back to sleep.

⌇

I make mistakes, clumsy moves, I get carried away, my hands hit and my mouth sometimes spits out ugly phrases. Monsieur Pozzo is moving into the top-floor apartment of a new building—but obviously also of very high standing—in the same neighborhood. The entire length of it has south-facing bay windows—an oven. It's too hot even for him. The elevator is wide enough for his electric wheelchair and me. But if a car parks on the very narrow sidewalk in front of the door, we can't get out.

One morning, at our usual café time, we're trapped. The car owner is standing there, talking to a guy on the side of the street. I tell him to move. Immediately.

"I'll just be one minute."

The minute goes by.

"You get your car out of here, now."

"One minute, I said!"

He's close to six feet, two inches, 220 pounds. I come up to his shoulder. I punch the hood of his car. It makes a dent just where the radiator is. He starts to curse me out. I get angry.

A few minutes later, on the way to the café, Monsieur Pozzo gives me a minimalist moral lecture, in his style.

"Abdel, you shouldn't have . . ."

It's true, and soon I'm back in court. The guy filed a formal complaint for battery and even furnished a medical certificate justifying an eight-day medical absence from work. I didn't have much trouble convincing the judge that a little guy like me, a life auxiliary to a tetraplegic person, could never have done all that to a guy this size. I've been discharged. Who's the best?

Maybe not me. Sometimes I carry Monsieur Pozzo and let him slip. Or I'm pulled down by his weight and can't get back on track. He hits his forehead. Or maybe I should say, I hit his forehead. I'm the only responsible party. A bump instantly appears, like an egg growing at high speed under his skin. Just like on Sylvester the cat's head when the mouse gives him a whack with a frying pan. I can't help laughing. I run to find a mirror, he has to see this before it disappears. Some days, he laughs with me. Others, not at all.

He says, "I can't take it anymore; I can't take being hurt anymore . . ."

And truly, sometimes Monsieur Pozzo has had enough. In his conferences, he never forgets to mention how you must never, never give in to discouragement. He can be proud of me: apart from his body, which I sometimes handle badly, I never give up on anything.

35

When TV producer and host Mireille Dumas suggested doing a special report on Philippe Pozzo di Borgo as well as our relationship, she contacted him first. She spoke to him like you do the Godfather, with deference and respect. It was 2002. He'd just published his first book, *Le Second Souffle* ("Second Wind"). He was the owner of his story and, more than that, of our story. The producer didn't directly consult the young Abdel Monsieur Pozzo talks about in his book—and not always in flattering terms. It's okay, it's not always about flattering me, I know that. I don't answer the phone when I don't recognize the number on the screen, I don't call back when I don't really like the voice on the answering machine, I expertly ignore the mail that crowds my mailbox.

It was Monsieur Pozzo himself who asked me to take part in the documentary about him. I gave the only answer possible when this man asks me a question, no matter what it is: yes.

Mireille and her team were very nice, and the experience didn't bother me. On the set of her show, *Vie privée, vie publique* ("Private Life, Public Life"), Monsieur Pozzo and I sat side by side, interviewed by the journalist as equals. I wasn't uncomfortable, but not really proud, either. I stared at the set décor; I tried to answer correctly, naturally, without mumbling, without forcing it. I heard myself say the word "friendship." Despite his insisting otherwise, I still used *vous*—the formal term for "you"—when talking to my "friend." I called him *monsieur*. For some reason I can't determine, I was incapable of calling him by his first name. It's still the case today, by the way.

The day after the show aired, the production team told us that they had an incredible peak in audience numbers for our report. I couldn't believe it, but still wasn't proud. As Pozzo rightly says, I'm "unbearable, vain, proud, brutal, fickle, human," but I'm not looking for glory. I wouldn't want to be recognized in the street and I can't see myself signing autographs. It's not about modesty: I don't have any. It's just that I didn't do anything to deserve admiration from strangers. I pushed a wheelchair, shock-anaesthetized a man whose sufferings seemed intolerable, I was his companion for a few painful years. Painful for him, not for me. I was, as he says, his "guardian demon." Honestly, it didn't cost me much. It even brought me a lot, and to use the same phrase that justifies the inexplicable: we aren't dogs, after all . . .

Recently, when several directorial teams planned to adapt our story to the big screen, one after the other, I didn't directly say yes. I was asked, obviously, but I could only give one answer: the same as the Godfather. I didn't ask to read the script, I didn't ask who'd be playing the role of the life auxiliary. I felt close to actor Jamel Debbouze, but I understood that he wasn't the man for the job. After the film was made, I realized I had a lot in things in common with Omar Sy, who portrayed me in the film: not only did he grow up in the projects at Mantes-la-Jolie, but he was raised by parents other than his own. He was also given as a present. I met him for the first time at Essaouira, where Khadija—Monsieur Pozzo's current companion—had organized a surprise party for Pozzo's sixtieth birthday. He sat next to me, very simple, open, natural. We talked just as if we'd always known each other.

The movie surprised me. During every scene up on the screen, I thought back to the moments as they actually happened. I saw myself at twenty-five again, with the cops, explaining to them that my boss was having an attack and that I had to get him to a hospital fast, a question of life or death! I wondered: Was I really that reckless? And why did he keep me? I don't think that he or I or anyone will ever be able to understand something so insane. When I rang his doorbell, I wasn't a generous guy yet. In fact, filmmakers Olivier Nakache and Eric Toledano created another me. Another Abdel, but better. They made my character the star of a film just as much as Philippe's, played by François Cluzet. It was clearly the best way to transform the drama into a comedy as well as to meet Monsieur Pozzo's wishes: to make people laugh at his situation in order to avoid pity and cheap sentiments.

I don't even think I signed a contract with the movie's production team. But why would I have? What did I, Abdel Yamine Sellou, give to them? A few jokes, at most. And even those jokes belong to Monsieur Pozzo because he's the one who elicited them. In real life, I'm not his equal partner; I have barely a second role, I'm almost an extra. I'm not being modest: I'm the best. But what I did really was easy.

After television, after film, the publishers approach me. Directly, this time. "We know Driss; now we want to know Abdel," they told me. I warned them: the little potbellied Arab is maybe not as nice as the tall black guy with pearly white teeth. They laughed; they didn't believe me. Too bad for them . . . I'm a gambler, I said *banco*. And so off I went to tell my story, in order, or almost. First Belkacem and Amina, whom I didn't always treat so well, I now realize. Only now, at more than forty, good job, Abdel . . . insolence, scheming, prison. That's good, Abdel, hold your head up high and proud. Tell them all: you can't get me! Finally, Monsieur Pozzo. Monsieur Pozzo finally and most important. Monsieur Pozzo, intelligence gained through dignity.

And suddenly, that's where it goes wrong.

Who am I to talk about him? I reassure myself, console myself, forgive myself: the things I've just told that are private are already in the film and in his book; he wanted it that way. He's the one who, after their first meeting, insisted that François Cluzet sit in on the personal care sessions that he goes through every day. The bedsores, the pieces of dead flesh that we cut with scissors, the catheter . . . You can't criticize the lack of modesty in a tetraplegic man: since he no longer controls his body, it doesn't belong to him anymore, it belongs to the doctors, the surgeons, the auxiliary nurses, the nurses, and even the life auxiliaries who take it away. It belongs to the actor who has to play the part, to the audience members asked to understand. To understand the moral of the story: that losing your physical autonomy isn't losing your life. That handicaps aren't strange animals that we can stare at without blushing, that there's no reason to avoid their gaze either.

But who am I to talk about suffering, modesty, and handicap? I just had better luck than the tons of blind people who had never seen anything before seeing *Intouchables*.

I put myself in the service of Philippe Pozzo di Borgo because I was young—young and stupid: I wanted to drive beautiful cars, travel first-class, sleep in châteaux, pinch rich women's asses, and laugh at their little offended squeals. I don't regret anything. Not my previous motivations, or the person I still am. But I became aware of something by telling my story in this book: that I finished growing up next to Monsieur Pozzo, from hope to an appetite for living, by way of the heart. Now it's my turn to be lyrical, like abstract art . . .

He offered his wheelchair for me to push like a crutch for me to lean on. I'm still using it today.

V

New Beginning

36

After a few years by his side, I had said enough to Monsieur Pozzo.

Crossing his arms over his stomach, leaning his torso forward, unfolding his limbs like the wrapper on a chocolate bar, putting him down in the right order, putting up his running shoes with the soles that will always be new . . . I had said enough. I needed to stop.

"Stop what? Abdel, are you leaving me?"

"No, I'll stay, but I can't consider it as my job. So I'll keep doing all of that, you can count on me, but you and me are going to do something else. We're going to be partners."

"Abdel, I'm the one who needs you. Not the other way around."

"Of course I need you! I'd like us to start a business together. I have the strength, the talk, but I don't have the manners. Paperwork, accounting, I don't know anything. The same goes for bowing to bankers. I don't know how to do it. You do."

"Bowing to bankers . . . my dear Abdel, you're overestimating my flexibility a little."

He came up with a great idea, so great that when launching it, I told everyone it was my own: car rentals to private clients with car delivery wherever they want. No more having to go to the agency: the client calls, gives an address, we take the keys to their door, and leave by our own means. The company will be called Téléloc, it'll belong to Monsieur Pozzo and him only, I'll just be there to learn.

To get started, the boss decides we won't use bankers.

"What do you mean? We're going to have to buy twenty cars, you know!"

"Don't worry, Abdel, I have some savings."

"Some savings! Oh, right, what do you call it already? An eggs . . ."

"An expression."

I love learning new words.

Monsieur Pozzo makes only one and unique condition to my presence in the company: that I never get behind the wheel of one of the rentals. Because I wrecked the Rolls-Royce, too. Once again, it wasn't my fault. The heat worked too well in the palace on four wheels, and Monsieur Pozzo was cold, as usual. We were driving at night toward the south of France, and it was easily 80 degrees inside the car. How could I have not fallen asleep? We heard a sort of *crack-boom* from the body of the car hitting the bumper on an old Golf. I also heard a second strange sound, more like a *chong*. That was the head of my passenger, thrown forward against the front seat. The rescue team arrived and first took care of me.

"Do you feel all right, sir?"

"Wonder . . ."

Then they went to look at the backseat. They opened the door, saw Monsieur Pozzo's body, and suddenly lost interest in me.

"There's a stiff in the back!"

Nice tact. I put Monsieur Pozzo back on the seat, dabbed the bump swelling on his temple, rigged the front of the car with a crowbar, and we got back on the road.

"Are you all right, Abdel? Did you fall asleep?"

"Not at all! That lady in front of us fishtailed!"

First chapter: Abdel is always right.

Second chapter: when Abdel is wrong, please refer to chapter one.

I never pretended to be in good faith.

We rent offices in Boulogne where we set up Téléloc. Three rooms. The first is used as a staff dormitory: Youssef, Yacine, Alberto, Driss. They're friends from the projects, from the pizzeria, Trocadéro. They don't all have papers—or driver's licenses, that goes without saying—they live there around the clock, the blankets pile up on the floor, coffee molds at the bottom of a mug, it always smells like mint tea. A second room serves as an office for Laurence, whom we've hired to take care of all the stuff requiring capable hands and a brain. The third room, which has a faucet, serves as a kitchen, bathroom . . . and doghouse for Youssef's two pit bulls, who water the carpet abundantly. In this environment, poor Laurence goes nuts.

"Abdel, you tell Youssef to take his dog to piss somewhere else or I quit!"

"Laurence, you wanted to do penance! It's now or never!"

She's got a sense of humor. She laughs.

The adventure lasts a few months. Enough time to send a few cars to the mechanic. To get complaints from clients: the cars arrive dirty, the tank empty, and the delivery people sometimes have the nerve to ask for a lift to Boulogne ... or somewhere else! Enough time to get complaints from the neighbors (the pit bulls water the elevator, too). The time for me to get picked up by the police.

"Abdel, you don't put clients in the trunk," Monsieur explains after getting me out.

The guy in question had rented a car and refused to give it back. I went to get him myself with Yacine. We only wanted to teach the thief a little lesson. By the way, he recognized that he was wrong because he didn't press charges.

"Abdel, this can't go on any longer. This company isn't Téléloc, it's Téléshock! Do you realize we're going to have to liquidate?"

~~

This Godfather is the big boss. He never threatens, never asks to see the books.

"Monsieur Pozzo, should we try something else?"

He's a gambler, maybe more so than me.

"Do you have an idea, Abdel?"

"Well ... the auctions, there's money in it, right?"

"Oh, not cars again!"

"No, I was thinking more about real estate auctions ... Candle auctions."

You had to find run-down apartments, renovate them,

and sell them fast, pocketing the added value in the process. In the United States, they call it "flipping." Unfortunately, Alberto, Driss, Yacine, Youssef, and his pit bulls were no more talented in plumbing and painting than they'd been in driving. Monsieur Pozzo quickly reoriented me toward an activity in which we could rely on just our own two skill sets. He also had another objective: a change of climate.

"Abdel, Paris doesn't suit me anymore. Too cold, too damp . . . you wouldn't happen to have a sunnier destination to propose, would you?"

"There's plenty of that. The West Indies? La Réunion? Brazil? Oh yeaaahhh . . . Brazil . . ."

I can see myself sipping a guava juice on a perfect beach surround by girls in thongs.

"Brazil is a bit far, Abdel. My children are grown, but I'd like to stay two or three hours away by plane, maximum. Say, what if we go and see what we could do in Morocco?"

"Morocco? Great, I love Morocco!"

It's true. I always preferred the couscous at Brahim's mother's place.

37

Monsieur Pozzo and I land in Marrakech. A mild breeze envelops us as we get off of the plane. We can already see the palm trees.

"That's good! Right, Monsieur Pozzo?"

"A limousine is waiting for us. Magnificent."

"That's nice! Right, Monsieur Pozzo?"

We go to the address my friend gave . . . a *riad,* a type of home with a garden or courtyard in the middle. It's locked, and I don't have the key.

"That's stupid! Right, Abdel?"

No problem. I know a place. Another *riad* in the Medina. The limousine drops us off at Jemaa-el-Fna plaza. The snake charmers back up when they see the wheelchair I'm dragging, more than pushing, over to the street. The ground is dirt. Pedestrians walk clinging to the wall on the right, bicycles race down the left lane, and we go right down the middle. We zigzag between chicken nests. Monsieur Pozzo is already regretting the trip. He regrets it even more when he realizes that the only room on the ground floor of the *riad* opens onto the patio and has no heating. I use my favorite joke:

"Don't move. I'm going to go get some electric heaters."

"I'm not moving Abdel, I'm not moving."

Turns out that I have a little mishap. It has to do with a fist—one of mine—thrown in the face of a not-so-helpful parking lot security guard. But when I finally come back, I've got what we need to transform the place into an oven. It's an emergency. Monsieur Pozzo's entire body is shaking.

"Well, you see, you're still moving!"

First thing the next day, we set out on a trek around the country. My driving talents are really put to the test. We get lost several times, but it's never my fault: we're not the ones who put so much snow in the Atlas and so much sand in the desert. Finally, we stop at Saïdia, otherwise known as "the blue pearl of the Mediterranean," in the extreme northeastern part of the country, just next to my native Algeria. A gorgeous beach, dozens of giant hotels, what else could you put here? Everything! We plan on creating an amusement park for tourists. We have to find the land and get the necessary authorization from the local governor, who is really hard to get in touch with. The days stretch out and not so effectively.

There's a very pretty young girl at the hotel where we're staying. When our eyes meet, something happens. Something new. Something that stops me. Right there. I am speechless. It reminds me now of the uneasiness I felt when I first showed up at Philippe Pozzo di Borgo's house.

I get a hold of myself. We're just passing through here.

"Abdel, you were just passing through on the avenue Léopold II, remember?" snickers the Jiminy Cricket in me. I shut him out, telling him to go bother Pinocchio. I must have been thinking out loud. The beautiful receptionist stares at me and bursts out laughing. She thinks I'm nuts. That's a bad start.

Monsieur Pozzo and I take our project very seriously, but it quickly becomes clear to us that it'll take months to get this started. We go back to Paris and bring Laurence into the project (once again, for anything that requires two capable hands and a brain). We multiply our round trips. We always stay at the same hotel, of course. Every time, the beautiful girl at reception smiles at me, attentive, distant, mysterious. I'm a total idiot around her.

She tells me, "I like you, Abdel Yamine."

And then: "I like you a lot, Abdel Yamine."

And finally: "If you want me, Abdel Yamine, you have to marry me."

There's something else . . . she's one of a gaggle of sisters. She's never had a big brother to shut her up; she lives her life as she pleases; she makes her own choices.

She asks Monsieur Pozzo: "Do you think it's a good idea for me to marry Abdel Yamine?"

He gives her his blessing like a father. But whose father? Hers or mine?

~

The beautiful girl's name is Amal. We have three children: Abdel Malek was born in 2005. I consider him the intellectual of the family: always well behaved, does well at school, and doesn't hit the younger ones too much. Our second son, Sala-heddine, came a year later. He had serious health problems at birth, had to have several serious operations, but he's a fighter. At home, we call him Didine, but he's more like Rocky Balboa. I see myself in him. I promise him a great career as a crook, which makes his mother crazy. Finally our daughter, Keltoum, came along in 2007. She has beautiful curly hair, is clever like a fox; she's charm and mischief all at once. I could have named her Candy. For now, Amal has decided we're stopping there. She calls the shots.

During a trip to Marrakech, Monsieur Pozzo met a rare pearl named Khadija. They live together in Essaouira, on the coast where it's never too hot or cold. They're raising two little girls whom they adopted. They're doing well. I go to see them a lot during vacation, either alone or with my family. All of the kids play together in the swimming pool; the house is filled with their screams and laughter. There's joy, there's life. If I drive on the Moroccan roads, I never drive very fast . . .

Our project for the amusement park in Saïdia never happened, but who cares.

38

I said enough to Monsieur Pozzo when I had my accident. I wasn't his employee anymore. I was still by his side. I still drove him wherever he needed to go. Every day I did all the things I had had to do over the preceding years, but I was no longer his life auxiliary. I was just in his life.

In October 1997, at the beginning of the November vacation, he asked me to take his son Robert-Jean to his grandmother's in Normandy. The kid got into the backseat, as quiet and nice as ever. Yacine wanted to get some air, so he sat next to me. I got behind the wheel of the Safrane, *my* Safrane. We didn't get very far: by Porte Maillot, just at the tunnel exit going toward La Défense, the car just quit. Engine failure, just like that, with no warning, right in the middle lane. I put on the hazards. At first the other cars honked at us before figuring out that we weren't trying to ruin their lives, then they drove around us in the right and left lanes. A highway safety truck got there fast.

Two men in fluorescent jumpsuits set up the roadblocks around the Safrane to guide traffic. Now we just had to wait.

Yacine and Robert-Jean stayed in the car. I leaned against the driver's side door and looked out for the tow truck. I wasn't worried; I didn't think I was in danger. For a good ten minutes, I watched the cars passing to the left a good eight feet in front of me, just beyond the bright orange cones showing them the way. Then I saw a semi also going around us on the left. Well, I saw the back of the truck that was approaching the Safrane and me. The driver turned a little too soon. I was sandwiched between his trailer and the Safrane. I just had time to shout. I sprawled out on the ground and lost consciousness for a moment.

I vaguely remember getting loaded into an ambulance. I felt an excruciating pain when they lifted me onto the gurney and I passed out again. I woke up at the hospital in Neuilly with the promise of surgery the next day. Philippe Pozzo di Borgo quickly dredged up a new life auxiliary. I can imagine how the poor guy must have felt being welcomed into his new job! His boss was asking him to drive him to the hospital to keep his predecessor company. They sent him in search of chocolate in the cafeteria to get rid of him.

"So how's the new guy?"

"He's . . . professional."

"He's not the king of bullshit, huh . . ."

"And you, Abdel, you're becoming the king of expressions!"

"Oh yeah . . . and who's the best?"

"You are, Abdel. You, when you're standing up!"

A hospital that doesn't give a shit about charity . . . you had to see it. The aristocratic tetraplegic and the little Arab with his hip in pieces, side by side in their wheelchairs checking out the nurses . . .

"How long will it be, Abdel?"

"A few weeks, at least. The doctors aren't sure the outcome will last very long. I don't need a prosthetic for now, but there's some problem with the ligament or something . . ."

"You're always welcome at home, you know that?"

"Of course, I'm the best!"

It's not always so easy to say thank you . . .

I got back to work, or back to my partnership with Monsieur Pozzo, a few months after the accident. That's when we started Téléloc, then the candle auction apartments, and finally the project in Morocco. During that period, I had to stop several times for surgery, not to mention weeks of physical rehabilitation. I wasn't even thirty yet. I thought I was a little young to be a part of the second class invalids, just one rank below Monsieur Pozzo. Social Security told me I wasn't allowed to work—too dangerous for my health! I thought that was a little extreme . . . that was proof that I'd already changed. But I never would have admitted it. As usual, I talked the talk without thinking about what I was saying.

"No more messing around, Abdel. You're going to find out what life is all about," Monsieur Pozzo told me.

"You're right, and I'm going to get all I can out of it! Now that I'm all broken, I'm going to get paid for doing nothing. The good life, here I come!"

He did everything he could to try to get me to pull it together. I tried hard to make him think he wasn't succeeding.

Being paid to stay at home was already boring to me: I couldn't sit still!

Monsieur Pozzo talked to me like a father would, an advisor, a sage. He tried to teach me order and morality, values that had always been completely foreign to me. He did it gently, with intelligence, so as not to put me on the defensive as I was with the teachers, the police, and the judges. He talked to me with kindness and detachment at the same time. He wanted me to obey the rules. It was surely partly to protect society, but mostly to protect me from it. He was afraid I'd put myself in danger, that I'd expose myself to the law again, to prison and also to my own violence. When I told him that I'd done time at Fleury-Mérogis it was in a moment of weakness or to show off. I don't know if he believed me or not, but he didn't question me about it. Ever since we first met, he'd known that I either didn't answer questions or gave ridiculous answers. He knew that you had to let me come forward on my own, and that I wouldn't necessarily do that anyway. He knew that I was uncontrollable, but he kept me on the tracks of acceptability. In his immobile hands, I was the puppet, the toy, the animal, the doll. Abdel Yamine Sellou, the first remote-control GI Joe in history.

39

When I talk about myself, I say what I want, when I want, if I
want. One truth hides a lie. Another truth seems so huge that
it seems like a lie. The lies add up and are so huge that you end
up wondering if they aren't hiding a certain truth . . . I tell the
truth, I tell a lie, you've got to be pretty smart to make out the
difference and hats off to the one who does. But sometimes I
get tricked. The journalists who interviewed me for Mireille
Dumas's show didn't get all the answers to their questions but
they knew how to get around the barrier created by my stubbornness. They filmed my silences. They did close-ups on my
face. They caught a look directed at Monsieur Pozzo. And these
images alone said a lot. A lot more than I would have admitted in words.

When I accepted the proposal to do this book, I naïvely
thought I could continue along the same road I'd always taken:
no cameras, no microphones this time. I say what I want, but I
shut up if I want! Before starting this exercise, I didn't realize I

was ready to talk. To explain to other people—the readers, as it happens—what I'd still never explained to myself. Once again, I'm talking about explaining, not "justifying." You understand by now that I'm all too happy to talk for self-satisfaction, but not for self-pity. I can't stand this fascination the French have with analyzing everything and forgiving everything, even the unforgivable, on the pretext of another culture, of a problem in upbringing, an unhappy childhood. I didn't have an unhappy childhood, on the contrary! I grew up like a lion in the savanna. I was the king. The strongest, most intelligent, and most seductive. When I let the gazelle drink at the watering hole, it was because I wasn't hungry. But when I was, I pounced on it. As a child, I wasn't scolded for being violent any more than a lion cub would be for his hunting instincts. Is that an unhappy childhood?

It was simply a childhood that didn't prepare me for becoming an adult. I wasn't aware of it and neither were my parents. Nobody's to blame.

I never talked about my past with Monsieur Pozzo. He tried, delicately, to get me to talk about it, but I'd launch into a joke. What he rightly heard was me refusing any kind of introspection, and he let it go. He was giving me chances without my knowing.

"Go back home and see your family."

"Get back in touch with the people who fed you."

"Go visit your native country."

And the most recent:

"Accept this proposal to write a book. It's an opportunity to take stock of your situation. It's worth it, you'll see!"

He knew what he was talking about. Before his accident, he had raced forward at two hundred miles an hour without ever looking back. Then from one day to the next, he was paralyzed, subjected to eighteen months of physical rehabilitation in a specialized center, surrounded by men and women just as unhappy as he was—and sometimes younger—and he took stock. He discovered who he really was deep down and learned to observe the Other—with a capital letter, as he says—he had not taken the time to see until then.

In my silence and in my jokes, Philippe Pozzo saw my refusal to slow down. He kept on encouraging me.

It took circumstances beyond my control to make me listen to his advice.

For starters, I went home to see my family. I visited my country.

40

I know the king in Morocco. I'm talking about Abdel Moula I,
king of turkeys. We're pretty close; we've helped each other out
before. We met under strange circumstances in the streets of
Paris. Life in his native country suits him much better.

Abdel Moula made me a golden offer. "You should get into
chicken! There's still room here in the poultry game."

He was ready to share his territory with me. I couldn't
accept. All feathered animals were the same to me, and I didn't
see myself being number two. Number one or nothing. Up
until then, I'd mostly been nothing at all—that had to change.
I also didn't see myself taking the place of a friend who'd welcomed me so generously. I simply didn't see myself in Morocco,
by the way: I was convinced that if the amusement park project in Saïdia didn't work out, it would be due in large part to
my origins. Algerians and Moroccans don't like each other
very much. Algerians think the Moroccans consider themselves
the princes of North Africa, full of their culture and riches. The

Moroccans think the Algerians are cowardly, lazy, rough. The Moroccan administration found every possible obstacle to stop me from marrying Amal. I had to bring her to France on a tourist visa to pull her out of her country's claws. Morocco wanted to keep Amal, but they didn't want me.

It quickly dawned on me that everything would be easier in Algeria and at least there, I wasn't betraying anyone. Abdel Moula offered to train me in poultry farming. From building construction to the choice of feed, he taught me everything. Monsieur Pozzo played the role of the banker. A very special banker who never counts. And I went to my native country to find a place to settle down.

It had been over thirty years since I set foot in Algeria. I'd forgotten all about its colors, its odors, and its sounds. But this wasn't some big "rediscovery." I had the impression of never having known the place. It was an introduction more than a reintroduction, and I was going there reluctantly.

Ever pragmatic, I stayed faithful to my creed: take advantage. I told myself that in France, everything had already been done, that the administrative formalities were very complicated, that banks didn't lend money (and definitely not to young Arabs with criminal records), that employer contributions were hefty even for start-ups . . . *Take advantage, Abdel, take advantage. You still have an Algerian passport, your country that you don't know is opening its arms, it's exempting you from contributions, income taxes, sales tax, and import costs for fifteen years.*

Take advantage . . . my creed, which Monsieur Pozzo called
"the Abdelian philosophy." I still think "philosophy" is a great
word . . .

I crisscross the country for weeks—from east to west, north to
south. I stop everywhere, in each city. I research the established
activities, the local population, the standards of living, the
unemployment rate. I explore the countryside, the state of the
roads leading to the fields, the factories, and the farms. I study
the competition. I don't go to Algiers. I don't look up the
address written on the back of the envelopes that, as a child, I
see sitting on the radiator in the entry. I have a good reason
not to go into the capital: you don't set up a poultry farm in
a big city! You need space so the birds can flap their wings and
air around them so that the nasty odors can evaporate. Finally,
I find the ideal spot—in Djelfa, three hundred thousand
inhabitants, the last big city before the desert. I take a few
more steps back to stay away from any homes, and plant my
flag. Well . . . I try.

To buy a plot of Algerian soil, you first have to prove that
you're truly a native. Furnish a birth certificate: I can't get a
hold of my father's family birth record. Provide an address: I
don't have a permanent address. Provide an identity card: for
that, you must furnish a birth certificate . . . I go back to France,
refusing to admit defeat, but I'm in a dark mood. Monsieur
Pozzo questions me and understands the problem right away.

"Abdel, there's no shame in asking for what's yours from
the one who brought you into this world."

He's right. There's no shame. No embarrassment. No joy. No enthusiasm. No impatience. No fear. There's nothing, no feeling. I feel nothing but indifference at the thought of being face-to-face with a man I haven't seen in over thirty years. My son Abdel Malek crawls up on my lap; he isn't walking yet.

I tell him, "I'm going to see grandfather. What do you think about that?"

Amal gently corrects me. "Grandfather lives next door to us. It's Belkacem . . ."

I had a hard time, despite my indifference . . . In Algiers, I met up with a friend from Beaugrenelle who was visiting family and I got him to get one of my brothers to come to a café without telling him I was there. Abdel Moumène, my younger brother by three years, was still a baby the last time I saw him. When he gets there, he immediately knows who he is dealing with. Aside from an inch or two and a few pounds, we could be twins.

"Abdel Yamine, it's really you! Wow! You're here? What are you doing here? And you come often? Wow! Come with me, I'm taking you to see our parents, they're going to be happy to see you."

I said no. Not this time. I have things to do. Another time, maybe.

"Don't tell them that you saw me."

I'm back one week later. I set up another meeting with Abdel Moumène at the café. He seems like a really nice guy.

"Listen, come home with me! What are you afraid of?"

Afraid of? Nothing! I almost popped him one.

I remembered the house. Everything came back to me when I walked in. My memory had played quite a trick on me. It bombarded me with images from the time of my birth up to my departure for France, when I was four. Where had all these memories gone for all those years downstairs at the projects, at Fleury-Mérogis, in Monsieur Pozzo's palaces? Where had they been hidden? In which corner of Abdel Yamine's bird brain—Abdel Yamine the rogue, the pickpocket, the thief . . . the auxiliary?

The image of an immense garden came back to me. It was a little concrete patio. The silhouette of a majestic medlar tree came back to me. The tree had no more fruit. The sensation of vastness came back to me. The living room could barely hold all of us.

We sat around a table. There was coffee, black and thick like tar, undrinkable. There was the father, the mother, the oldest sister, two other girls, Abdel Moumène, and me. Abdel Ghany was the only one missing (he lives in Paris with his wife and their children; he's happy). We looked at each other a lot without talking very much. Just a few words. No blame, acknowledgment.

"You didn't write to us very much."

To avoid saying nothing at all.

"You didn't call us very often."

An expression!

"How is your wife?"

I found they knew everything about my life from Belkacem and Amina.

"We saw you on the television, in the movie with the handicapped man."

The handicapped man. Monsieur Pozzo. He was far away . . .

I told them that I was looking for a piece of land in the south to start a poultry farm. That maybe—it wasn't definite yet, but maybe—I was going to settle down there. Not very far. I gave them a little information about my plans but didn't go into the details. They listened to me without responding; they didn't give their opinion, or ask for anything more. While I was talking to them, questions popped into my head, one after the other, and I didn't understand why they weren't asking them: Why now? Why so late? And what do you want from us? What do you expect?

Nothing.

They must have known, that's why they weren't saying anything.

⟿

I looked at the furniture—simple, oriental couches with their shiny, colored cushions lined up neatly. I looked at Abdel Moumène and all of his sisters who live with Mom and Dad and don't do much with their days. I looked at this man with dry, light eyes, as blue as the Mediterranean, a color I didn't inherit. I looked at this woman, her black hair, dyed with henna, her European shirt, her stomach that I came out of thirty-five years earlier. I took stock of all the members of this family. I was the shortest, the fattest, had the biggest feet and shortest fingers out of all of them. I'm Gizmo from the Gremlins. Danny DeVito next to Arnold Schwarzenegger. At Beaugrenelle, people often said I looked like my father. They were trying to be nice, to please me. They didn't know.

I thought that by sending me to Paris, my parents had given me better chances in life than I would have had in Algiers, in this modest house, in the shadow of a scrawny medlar tree, surrounded by a gaggle of brothers and sisters. In this country where we don't push the baby birds from the nest so they can fly higher. In this country where I never could have met a man like Philippe Pozzo di Borgo.

I am able to buy the land at Djelfa and I hire eight men who seem to be honest, more or less. Together we install a generator, build the buildings, and get the business started. Every three or four weeks, I go back to Paris to see Amal and the children, who are in school in France. They have their friends and their routines there. In Djelfa, I sleep in my office. And when I'm going to spend a few days in Algiers, I sleep in Abdel Moumène's room.

There will always be people to judge me. And therefore to sentence me, without the slightest hesitation. I'll always be the little Arab who takes advantage of the weakness of a heavily handicapped man. I'll always be a hypocrite, a guy with no manners who doesn't respect anything or anyone, a narcissist who, not satisfied with being on the television, publishes his memoir at the age of forty. But I don't give a damn about what people might think about me. I can look at myself in the mirror.

Monsieur Pozzo says that I'm more at peace because I've found my place in society. Just a few years ago, he thought me capable of killing a guy "in a fit of rage," in his words. He added that he'd bring me oranges in prison, like any father would for his incarcerated son. I don't consider him a father. May he forgive me, but the concept of a father in my little story is still fairly unclear . . . He isn't less than a father, he isn't more, he's simply himself, Monsieur Pozzo di Borgo, and I have to hold myself back from writing his name in all capitals, the *di* included.

～

He's the one who taught me to read. Not to decipher, but read. The one who caught me up on part of my lack of education. Before I knew him, I got a kick out of saying I had a negative-six-year degree. Now I've maybe got a negative-one-year degree, I don't know. He's the one who taught me humility, and there was a lot of work to do there. The one who opened my eyes to the middle and upper classes, an alien world where some of the inhabitants aren't so bad after all. He's the one who taught me to think before answering, and even before acting. He is the one who encouraged me to throw away the mask. The one who told me *yes, yes Abdel, you're the best*, even though I was far from being convinced of it despite whatever I might have said. The one who raised me. Who took me higher. To become better. And even do a pretty decent job as a father.

～

Last summer, I took my children for a ride on the Seine in a Bateau-Mouche. We sat with the tourists, who've changed since the days when I robbed them. There were a lot of Chinese, fully equipped in terms of technology, nice stuff that would bring a nice sum at the flea market in Montreuil. There were quite a few Russians, too, beautiful girls for sure, but only skin and bones—not my type—and guys a lot bigger built than me. I wouldn't have gotten into it with them. Abdel Malek asked me intelligent questions, as usual.

"Papa, what's that building? It looks like a train station."

I surprise myself by talking like a book.

"It was a train station in the past, you're right. Now, it's a museum. It's called Orsay. There are paintings inside. Lots of paintings."

I thought I was being too serious. It wasn't me. I had to add something.

"You know, Abdel Malek, they didn't have cameras before, that's why people painted . . ."

My son again, a little farther on:

"And that bridge, why is it cut in two?"

"Oh . . . the Pont Neuf! It's divided in two because it links the tip of the Ile de la Cité to both river banks of Paris."

"Is there a city on Ile de la Cité? A city like Beaugrenelle?"

"Uh . . . no, there's the Palais de Justice! That's where they judge people and decide to send them to prison when they do bad things."

"Like you, Papa!"

This time, it's Salaheddine who speaks up. My miniature clone. And very proud of his father, of course.

The boat took us farther. The children talked to me about the ocean we were sailing on. I explained the difference between an ocean, a stream, and a river to them. Well . . . I wasn't so sure about the part where the source is born in the mountains. We passed by the bottom of XVIth district. I showed them where I lived when I was little like them, but they didn't care a bit.

"And that statue, it looks like the Statue of Liberty. What is she doing? Why is she lifting her arm like that?"

"She's trying to find a network for her BlackBerry Torch . . ."

They laughed, but they didn't believe me. I told them that Papa didn't know many things because he didn't pay good attention to the teacher at school.

"Philippe will know! You can just call him, right?"

"Monsieur Pozzo, yes, he'd definitely know, Monsieur Pozzo . . ."

I have two fathers, two mothers, an ebony black avatar in the movies, a wife, two sons, and a daughter. I always had buddies, sidekicks, and accomplices. Monsieur Pozzo is perhaps simply a friend. The first one. The only one.